BECOMING

A WOMAN

OF *strength*

BECOMING
A WOMAN
OF *strength*

*"The eyes of the LORD search the whole
earth in order to strengthen those whose
hearts are fully committed to him."*
2 CHRONICLES 16:9

CYNTHIA HEALD

NAVPRESS
Discipleship Inside Out®

NAVPRESS
Discipleship Inside Out®

NavPress is the publishing ministry of The Navigators, an international Christian organization and leader in personal spiritual development. NavPress is committed to helping people grow spiritually and enjoy lives of meaning and hope through personal and group resources that are biblically rooted, culturally relevant, and highly practical.

For a free catalog go to www.NavPress.com
or call 1.800.366.7788 in the United States or 1.800.839.4769 in Canada.

ISBN-13: 978-1-61521-620-8

Some of the anecdotal illustrations in this book are true to life and are included with the permission of the persons involved. All other illustrations are composites of real situations, and any resemblance to people living or dead is coincidental.

Unless otherwise identified, all Scripture quotations in this publication are taken from the *Holy Bible*, New Living Translation (NLT), copyright © 1996, 2004. Used by permission of Tyndale House Publishers, Inc., Wheaton, Illinois 60189. All rights reserved. Other versions used include: the New King James Version (NKJV). Copyright © 1982 by Thomas Nelson, Inc. Used by permission. All rights reserved; THE MESSAGE (MSG). Copyright © 1993, 1994, 1995, 1996, 2000, 2001, 2002. Used by permission of NavPress Publishing Group; the *Holy Bible, New International Version*® (NIV®), Copyright © 1973, 1978, 1984 by Biblica, used by permission of Zondervan, all rights reserved; the New American Standard Bible® (NASB), Copyright © 1960, 1962, 1963, 1968, 1971, 1972, 1973, 1975, 1977, 1995 by The Lockman Foundation. Used by permission; the *Amplified Bible* (AMP), © The Lockman Foundation 1954, 1958, 1962, 1964, 1965, 1987; and the Holman Christian Standard Bible (HCSB)® Copyright © 2003, 2002, 2000, 1999 by Holman Bible Publishers. All rights reserved.

Printed in the United States of America

3 4 5 6 7 8 / 17 16 15 14 13

CONTENTS

Suggestions for Using This Study 7

Introduction 9

The Father and the Child 14

Chapter 1 God, the Great Giver of Strength 15

Chapter 2 His Strength in Our Weakness 25

Chapter 3 Strong Enough to Be Teachable 35

Chapter 4 Strong Enough to Wait 47

Chapter 5 Strong Enough to Exercise Self-Control 59

Chapter 6 Strong Enough to Be Holy 71

Chapter 7 Strong Enough for Spiritual Warfare 83

Chapter 8 Strong Enough to Be Bold 99

Chapter 9 Strong Enough to Be Christ's Bondslave 111

Chapter 10 Strong Enough to Persevere 123

Chapter 11 Clothed with Strength 135

The Father and the Child 148

Notes 149

About the Author 157

SUGGESTIONS FOR USING THIS STUDY

This study is designed for both individual and small-group use, and for women of any age or family status.

Many of the questions will guide you into Scripture passages. Ask God to reveal His truth to you through His Word. Bible study references — such as commentaries and handbooks — can help you understand particular passages by providing historical background, contexts, and common interpretations. (In a few cases, you may want to access a standard dictionary for general word definitions.)

Other questions will ask you to reflect on your own life. Approach these questions honestly and thoughtfully; however, if you're doing this study in a group, don't feel that you must reveal private details of your life experiences. Use the "Reflection" questions at the close of each chapter to help you work through significant issues raised by your study. If you keep a personal journal, you might want to write these reflections there rather than in this book.

The quotations from classic thinkers and writers have been carefully selected to enhance your understanding and enjoyment of the content in *Becoming a Woman of Strength*. The references for these quotations (see the "Notes" section at the back of the book) will also furnish an excellent reading list for your own devotional reading and study.

Most facilitators stimulate discussion by moving through each chapter section by section and by using the personal application questions placed throughout the study. Providing time for prayer along with a loving and safe environment for women to share their personal insights and challenges will hopefully encourage, unite, and bless each member of the group.

There is also a DVD curriculum available as a companion for small-group use.

INTRODUCTION

God delivered the Israelites from slavery in Egypt and under the leadership of Moses was guiding them to His chosen land for them — Canaan. Twelve spies were sent to explore the land and bring back a report. Ten of the spies made this observation: "We entered the land you sent us to explore, and it is indeed a bountiful country — a land flowing with milk and honey. . . . But the people living there are powerful, and their towns are large and fortified. We even saw giants there, the descendants of Anak!" . . . "*We can't go up against them! They are stronger than we are!*" (Numbers 13:27-28,31, emphasis added).

Every time I read this passage, I wish I could have been there to shout, "Stop! Don't you understand that when you trust God and He is leading you, the strength of giants is inconsequential compared to the strength of God! If you don't go into Canaan, you'll forfeit God's plan for you and you'll miss seeing God's might and glory manifested against the massive walls of Jericho!" (see Joshua 6:20).

What God wanted the Israelites to know was that it was *His* strength that would go before them to defeat giants and bring down walls. They still had to enter the land and fight, but His enabling would give the victory. They were not to depend upon their strength, but His. They were not to look at giants, but at their God. The Lord is still teaching this truth today. He longs to show Himself mighty on our behalf; He longs to be our source of strength. He wants us to believe the Scripture, "Human strength can't begin to compete with God's 'weakness'" (1 Corinthians 1:25, MSG).

Before you begin *Becoming a Woman of Strength*, I want to highlight two key verses that are essential to this study. The first verse, Ephesians 3:16, is the "heart" of the study:

I pray that from his glorious, unlimited resources he will empower you with inner strength through his Spirit.

Our strength is an inner strength, a *heart* strength, given to us through the Holy Spirit. Paul's prayer is all-inclusive — strength for whatever we need. The biblical commentator T. Croskery noted,

> It is a prayer that God would make us eminent in grace and goodness, that our souls may prosper and be in health like our bodies, that we may be able to grapple with all our spiritual enemies, to resist temptation, to endure afflictions, to perform the duties of our Christian calling. If we have strength, we shall be able to run in the way of God's commandments. Our physical strength is renewed from day to day by food and rest. So is our spiritual strength daily renewed by the Bread of life; and thus the apostle could say of himself, "I can do all things through Christ which strengtheneth me."[1]

The second verse, Philippians 4:13, is based on the apostle's proclamation and is the "hand" of the study. Our strength is a *doing* strength given to us through the Holy Spirit.

> I have strength for all things in Christ Who empowers me [I am ready for anything and equal to anything through Him Who infuses inner strength into me; I am self-sufficient in Christ's sufficiency]. (Philippians 4:13, AMP)

Paul penned these heartfelt words in a letter to the church in Philippi. In it he praised them for their concern for him and shared with them a valuable lesson he had learned — a secret for living in every situation. He discovered that he could be content with whatever he had in his present circumstances. Whether he was rich or poor, full or hungry, he could be satisfied, at peace, and untroubled. In fact, the truth of the sufficiency of Christ so gripped his heart that he exclaimed, *"I can do everything through Christ, who gives me strength."*

The verb "to strengthen" is from the Greek word *endunamoō*. It is contracted from *en*, meaning "in," and *dunamoō*, meaning "to make strong." Contracted together they mean "to empower, enable, (increase in) strength." It is a present and continued act.[2]

Matthew Henry paraphrased the verse in this way: "Through Christ, who is strengthening me, and does continually strengthen me; it is by his constant and renewed strength I am enabled to act in every thing; I wholly depend upon him for all my spiritual power."[3]

These two verses anchor our study and permeate every chapter. They are commanding truths that provide hope and focus our attention on Christ. W. F. Adeney observed, "In Christ the heaviest burden may be borne and the hardest task accomplished and the weakest soul win the victory over the most powerful foe, with a strength which is practically omnipotent, because it is derived from an almighty source."[4]

Complementing these key Scriptures and giving insight on God's part and our part in becoming women of strength is this teaching from Jerry Bridges: "We need to learn this scriptural principle that the Holy Spirit works in us to enable us to live lives pleasing to God. He does not do the work for us; rather, He enables us to do the work. . . . As I depend on Him, He enables *me to* live a life pleasing to Him."[5]

We are empowered by an inner strength in order to *do* the Lord's will. The apostle Paul stated it this way to the Corinthian church: "It was God giving me the work to do, God giving me the energy to do it" (1 Corinthians 15:10, MSG). To his disciple Timothy he wrote, "I thank Christ Jesus our Lord, who has given me strength to do his work" (1 Timothy 1:12).

This study is not only about understanding our weaknesses and God's desire to strengthen us for His purposes, but also about realizing our inclination to rely on our own strength and insight in making decisions and handling difficulties. This study is about giving up our independence ("No, Lord, we will not go into Canaan") and learning to depend wholly upon the Lord ("Yes, Lord, because You are my strength, I can conquer Canaan"). Our need is to grasp this profound truth declared by Croskery: "That God reveals himself to us as the great Giver of strength."[6]

The last section of each chapter will give you an opportunity to take time for reflection in order to help you solidify what you have learned and to help you come away with a new insight or practical application.

I live in the desert. One day as I was unloading groceries and going back and forth from the car to the kitchen, our cat, Black, brought in a rather large lizard and placed it in the center of our living room. Black had already bitten this poor creature and its back was bloody. I stood there looking at this pitiful, unappealing animal knowing that I had to pick it up and take it outside. I prayed, "Okay, Lord, I can do this." This heartfelt but short prayer is my *Reader's Digest* version of Philippians 4:13. Implied in the prayer is my dependence upon the Lord to strengthen me for whatever task is at hand. So praying all the way, I took a deep breath, got a paper towel, picked up the lizard, and took it out of the house.

I know that this incident is rather inconsequential, but for me it illustrates the principle that no matter what we are facing, we can be strengthened to do what is needed. My desire is that we will begin to live the truth of Ephesians 3:16 and Philippians 4:13 — that *whatever* challenges we encounter (lizards included), we can handle them because of the Lord's strength dwelling within us. Our weaknesses really do not enter into the equation. In fact, it is our very weakness that God uses to make us strong. I pray that as a result of completing this study, you will join with me in praying one of my continual prayers: "Okay, Lord, I can do this."

> I ask — ask the God of our Master, Jesus Christ, the
> God of glory — to make you intelligent and discerning

in knowing him personally, your eyes focused and clear, so that you can see exactly what it is he is calling you to do, grasp the immensity of this glorious way of life he has for his followers, oh, the utter extravagance of his work in us who trust him — endless energy, boundless strength!

Ephesians 1:17-19, MSG

All of our praise rises to the One who is strong enough to make *you* strong.

Romans 16:25, MSG

The Father and the Child

The child spoke:

Father, life is not always easy.

I know, My child, My kingdom has not come in full power.

There is much to deal with — heartache, disease, disappointment, hard times. Often I feel weak and overwhelmed.

Remember My Son's words: "Here on earth you will have many trials and sorrows. But take heart, because I have overcome the world" (John 16:33).

I know, Lord, but sometimes I forget and try to overcome the world on my own. Daily I find that I am so inconsistent in handling situations and difficulties. There are times when I feel helpless and call out to You, and other times I think I can handle things by myself. It seems that when I think I'm strong enough to take care of a problem, I usually end up stressed and frustrated. What am I doing wrong?

It grieves Me to see My children choose to live without the strength that I can give.

But I feel that I need to be strong for You.

Yes, you are to be strong, but you must understand that My strength is perfected in your weakness. Your strength must come from Me; I am the source of your strength.

And how do I learn to rely on You and not myself?

Take My Hand and with your eyes, see, and with your ears, listen to My Word. You must learn to rely on Me and know that it is My joy to strengthen you with power through My Spirit in your inner being.

CHAPTER ONE

GOD, THE GREAT GIVER OF STRENGTH

The eyes of the LORD search the whole earth in order to strengthen those whose hearts are fully committed to him.

2 CHRONICLES 16:9

Am I prepared to let God grip me by His power and do a work in me that is worthy of Himself?[1]

OSWALD CHAMBERS

Mary Slessor — A Woman Strengthened by God

Born in 1848 outside of Aberdeen, Scotland, Mary was raised by a godly, loving, and devoted mother, and by a father who spent the majority of his salary consuming alcohol. At age eleven Mary left school and worked ten hours a day for fourteen years as a weaver in a factory. Sensing that her background of self-denial, heartaches, and hardships had prepared her to serve the Lord in the hardest of places, Mary offered her services to the United Presbyterian Church of Scotland, and in 1876 she set sail for missionary service in Calabar, now Nigeria. When told "that Calabar was the white man's grave," Mary said, "but it is also a post of honor. Since few volunteer for that section, I wish to go because my Master needs me there."[2] While working at the mission in Calabar she encountered "superstitions, cruelty, suffering and belief in repulsive gods."[3] She was appalled to learn that twin newborns, believed to be evil spirits, were routinely killed, and their mothers exiled to the jungle to die. Mary sought to put a stop to this practice by explaining Jesus' love for children. She also took a pair of twins into her own home to show that she suffered no evil effects.

After twelve years of ministering in the Calabar region, she moved to live among the natives of Okoyong, whom the world called "impossibles." Mary was warned that the natives were extremely cruel and that she was courting death, but "her heart was brave and strong, for God had surcharged it with an overflowing love for the heathen, and whatever the difficulties, she knew she must succeed through Christ who loved her and gave Himself for her redemption."[4] Although she suffered from chronic malarial infection, Mary fiercely confronted barbaric practices, courageously interceded and stood her ground between warring chiefs, tirelessly dealt with drunkenness among the natives, and boldly trusted God to heal and defeat the evil practices of the witch doctors.

For thirty-eight years she trekked through jungles barefoot; lived near poisonous swamps; climbed hills; built schools, churches, and rest homes; and opened trade opportunities. At Okoyong she was even appointed as their magistrate and presided over the native court. She was continually "building, cementing, painting, varnishing, teaching, preaching, healing. . . . Her hands were hard and rough and often bled from too much heavy outdoor work. The skin of her palms was gone and her nails were worn to the quick. But in describing the pitifully clad Mary Slessor, a newspaper reporter wrote, 'She conquered me if she did not convert me.'"[5]

To Mary, all her tasks were sacred and offered to the Lord as part of her service. Living in isolation from like-hearted companionship, she had a vital relationship with the Lord. While Mary was visiting in Scotland, a woman asked how she attained her intimacy with God.

Mary replied, "Ah, woman, when I am out there in the bush I have often no other one to speak to but my Father, and I just talk to Him."[6]

This diminutive missionary was revered by the natives and lovingly named "White Ma" whom Christ had made the conqueror of cannibals. Her well-marked Bible revealed her love and understanding of the God she so faithfully served. Here are a few excerpts: "God is never behind time. . . . The smallest things are as absolutely necessary as the great things. . . . Blessed the man and woman who is able to serve cheerfully in the second rank — a big test. . . . An arm of flesh never brings power."[7]

God Strengthens Those Loyal to Him

1. a. In stating "An arm of flesh never brings power," Mary Slessor was likely echoing King Hezekiah's words concerning the threat of a foreign king: "With him is an arm of flesh; but with us is the LORD our God, to help us and to fight our battles" (2 Chronicles 32:8, NKJV).

Our key verse for this chapter, 2 Chronicles 16:9, also implies God's eagerness to fight for us. It is interesting, though, to study the context of this Scripture.

Read 2 Chronicles 16:1-10 and write down the circumstances in which Hanani, the seer, spoke these words to King Asa.

623 Because you relied on the king of Aram & not on the Lord the army of Aram has escaped.

b. In Hanani's faithful reproof of Asa, he mentioned God's deliverance of Judah from the Ethiopians. Read 2 Chronicles 14:8-13 and record how Asa responded when he felt helpless and weak.

621 He called on the Lord. "We rely on you Do not let men prevail against us.

c. These scriptural accounts depict two entirely different responses from Asa when he was faced with adversity. As you meditate on his choices, write down why you think we are inclined to call on God in one situation but feel the need to rely on human effort in another circumstance.

Has he not helped us in six troubles? And have we any reason to suspect him in the seventh? But see how deceitful our hearts are! We trust in God when we have nothing else to trust to, when need drives us to him; but, when we have other things to stay on, we are apt to stay too much on them and to lean to our own understanding as long as that has any thing to offer; but a believing confidence will be in God only, when a smiling world courts it most.[8]

Matthew Henry

2. Our reliance on "flesh" pales in comparison to the power and might of our God whose strength is proclaimed throughout Scripture. Write down what you discover about God's strength from the following passages.

1 Chronicles 29:10-12

841   Psalm 89:5-13

Almighty

1633   1 Corinthians 1:25

the foolishness of God is wiser than man's wisdom & the weakness of God is stronger than man's strength.

1764   1 John 4:4 *The one who is in you is greater than the one who is in the world.*

> Because the Holy Spirit is so mighty, attempt nothing without Him. Do not begin a project, or carry on an enterprise, or conclude a transaction without imploring His blessing. Honor Him by acknowledging your entire weakness apart from Him.[9]
>
> *Charles Spurgeon*

God's Vigilance for the Wholehearted

3. a. "For His eyes are on the ways of man, and He sees all his steps" (Job 34:21, NKJV). How do these verses illustrate God's vigilance and care for us?

766   Psalm 11:4

He observes the sons of men his eyes examine them.

785 Psalm 33:13-19

He delivers us from our tr...

786 Psalm 34:15-19

He delivers us from our troubles

b. It is almost beyond our grasp to comprehend God's faithful watch over His creation. How does the knowledge of God's observation encourage and motivate you?

He strengthens me to know that I can always rely on him to be there.

---

4. a. The prophet Daniel was captured by the pagan Babylonians and later appointed to serve in a governing position. Daniel had many occasions when he needed to depend upon the Lord. As you read Daniel 6:1-23, write down why you believe God strengthened Daniel's heart.

b. God strengthens those whose hearts are *fully committed* to Him. In light of studying Daniel's commitment to God, how would you describe your devotion and commitment to the Lord?

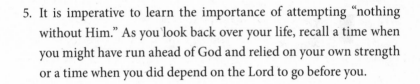

Consecration is the voluntary set dedication of one's self to God, an offering definitely made, and made without any reservation whatever. . . . The consecration which meets God's demands and which he accepts is to be full, complete, with no mental reservation, with nothing withheld. . . . It involves our whole being, all we have and all that we are. Everything is definitely and voluntarily placed in God's hands for his supreme use.[10]

E. M. Bounds

---

5. It is imperative to learn the importance of attempting "nothing without Him." As you look back over your life, recall a time when you might have run ahead of God and relied on your own strength or a time when you did depend on the Lord to go before you.

The only strength used in God's battles is the strength He alone imparts.[11]

Charles Spurgeon

Thoughts from an Older Woman

The key verse for this chapter, 2 Chronicles 16:9, is one of my favorites — at least the first sentence is. But there are two other sentences in this verse, and I purposely did not use them because they carry a strong rebuke and they are certainly not as grand and encouraging as part "a." But part "b" — *"What a fool you have been! From now on you will be at war."* — is an integral part of the verse and must be acknowledged. In fact, it must be taken to heart.

We are indeed foolish to rely on our strength when we are faced with difficulty. To try to "fix" our trials without the Lord is unwise and foolhardy, and there are consequences in doing things "my" way. I wonder how many times I have missed out on God's plan of deliverance for me because I was in a hurry and thought I knew best?

Dear Sarai, Abram's wife, thought she knew how to fulfill God's promise of a son. She, like King Asa, took matters into her own hands and relied on her own insight and strength to overcome her barrenness. Sarai decided that she would "help" God out in getting a son by giving her maid, Hagar, to Abram. She ran ahead of God and suffered the turmoil and repercussions of a rebellious servant and a "son" who eventually had to be sent away (see Genesis 16). If only she had waited, if only she had taken time to seek the Lord for His will before influencing Abram, if only she had not relied on her own strength.

Years ago — BCP (before cell phones) — I was flying from Tucson to meet my elderly mother in Los Angeles for a barbershop quartet convention. She was flying from Houston, and we were to meet in the baggage claim area. My flight from Tucson to Phoenix was delayed, and anxiety filled my heart for I realized it would be impossible to make my connecting flight. I was beside myself trying to figure out how I could get word to my mom. I pictured her wondering where I was and not knowing what to do. In the midst of my distress, I cried out to God asking Him to give her peace and petitioning Him to go before me and help me.

I was so emotional and in such a hurry that as I stepped off the plane onto the jetway, I almost missed the airline agent holding up a sign that said, "If you are flying to Los Angeles, please stay here with me." Several of us crowded around him, and then he led us down the outside stairway to a waiting van that whisked us across the tarmac to the plane flying to LA. On our way, he told us that our bags would also be on the plane. *I couldn't believe it.* I am a frequent flyer, and I had never experienced this airline courtesy. As I sat there in the van, tears of gratitude trickled down my cheeks. I also couldn't believe that I had allowed myself to spend the last hour and a half overly anxious and apprehensive. How foolish I had been. It never entered my mind that the airline would or could do what they were doing. Actually it never entered my mind that God might be searching the skies of Arizona desiring to "grip me by His power." I was overwhelmed that God would personally intercede and fight this little battle for me, that He would strengthen my heart and give me victory. I was an incredibly grateful child; I still am.

REFLECTION
Strengthened Through His Spirit to Rely on God's Strength

Mary Slessor exemplifies a woman who was wholeheartedly devoted to God; she was empowered with inner strength and her roots went down deep into God's love and she was kept strong. She is proof that God searches the whole earth to strengthen those whose hearts are fully committed to Him, and it is true that we really can depend on His strength to do all things through Christ.

During the next few days, be diligent to voluntarily place yourself in God's hands. Pray for Him to strengthen your spirit's sensitivity to the promptings of His Holy Spirit as He pinpoints areas in your life where you are prone to rely on your own strength. (His promptings may come through His Word, a thought in your heart, or through another person.)

You might want to begin to keep a "Strength Journal" as you go through this study. For this chapter record in your journal the promptings He gives you as you become more alert to the times you rely on your own strength. As you reflect on this chapter, write a prayer asking God to show you how you can become more wholehearted in your relationship to Him. Let Him know of your desire to become more dependent upon His strength. Ask Him to grip you by His power so that He can begin to do a work in you that is worthy of Himself. You might close your prayer by expressing your gratefulness to Him for being the great Giver of strength.

 PRAYER THOUGHT

Okay, Lord, I can do this: Empowered by Your Spirit, I will attempt nothing without You, for I can do everything through Christ, who gives me strength.

Happy are those who hear the joyful call to worship,
    for they will walk in the light of your presence, LORD.
They rejoice all day long in your wonderful reputation.
    They exult in your righteousness.
You are their glorious strength.
    It pleases you to make us strong.
                Psalm 89:15-17, emphasis added

SUGGESTED SCRIPTURE MEMORY: 2 Chronicles 16:9

CHAPTER TWO

*H*IS *S*TRENGTH IN *O*UR *W*EAKNESS

Each time he said, "My grace is all you need. My power works best in weakness." So now I am glad to boast about my weaknesses, so that the power of Christ can work through me.

2 CORINTHIANS 12:9

Are you mourning over your weakness? Take courage! You must be conscious of weakness before the Lord gives you the victory. Your emptiness is the preparation for being filled with God's strength. Being cast down is the making ready for your lifting up:
   When I am weak then am I strong.
   Grace is my shield and Christ is my song.[1]

CHARLES SPURGEON

Doug Nichols — God's Strength in Weakness

Doug and Margaret Nichols, missionaries for forty years, spent most of their lives ministering in the Philippines. They currently reside in Seattle, where Doug serves as founder and international director emeritus with

Action International Ministries. Doug travels extensively throughout the world speaking on behalf of missions.[2]

The Nicholses have faced their share of obstacles, but one major difficulty greatly impacted their lives. After surgery for colon cancer, Doug was told that he had a 30 percent survival rate. A year of radiation and chemo left him weak, and he and his wife knew that the end might be drawing near. Although this couple was going through deep waters, their attention was diverted by the alarming news from Rwanda of the civil war and of the incredible carnage that forced many Rwandans to flee across the border only to live in filthy, ill-equipped refugee camps where cholera was taking a heavy toll. Like many Americans, Doug wanted to do something for this country — hold children, offer hope, do a little something to help. Soon he was traveling with a team of doctors and nurses into the heart of Rwanda.

A Rwandan Christian leader whom Doug knew had hired three hundred refugees as stretcher bearers to carry the wounded to the doctors and to bury the dead. One day the leader approached Doug: "We have a problem. I was given only so much money to hire these people, and now they want to go on strike." Doug replied, "But if they don't work, thousands will die. Can I talk with them?" The leader shrugged his shoulders, saying, "It won't do any good. They want more money. They are angry. Who knows what they might do?"

After calling the workers together, Doug walked over to an old burned-out school building and, standing beside an interpreter, began to speak: "I can't possibly understand the pain you've experienced, and now seeing your wives and children dying of cholera, I can never understand how that feels. Maybe you want more money for food and water and medical supplies for your families. I've never been in that position either. Nothing tragic has ever happened in my life that compares to what you've suffered. The only thing that's ever happened to me is that I've got cancer."

He was about to go on when the interpreter stopped. "Excuse me," he said, "did you say cancer?"

"Yes."

"And you came over here? Did your doctor say you could come?"

"He told me that if I came to Africa, I'd probably be dead in three days."

"Your doctor told you that and you still came? What did you come for? And what if you die?"

"I'm here because God led us to come and do something for these people in His name. I'm no hero. If I die, just bury me out in that field where you bury everybody else."

To Doug's amazement the interpreter began to weep. With tears he spoke to the crowd, "This man has cancer." Suddenly everyone grew very quiet. In Rwanda, cancer is an automatic death sentence. "He came over here willing to die for our people," the interpreter continued, "and we're going on strike just to get a little money? We should be ashamed."

Instantly men on all sides began falling to their knees in tears. Dumbfounded, Doug watched as people then stood to their feet, walked over to their stretchers, and quietly went back to work.

Later Doug reflected, "What did I do? Nothing. It wasn't my ability to care for the sick. It wasn't my ability to organize. All I did was get cancer. But God used that very weakness to move the hearts of people. So many are discouraged by weakness. We feel that God could never use us; we have nothing to offer. . . . You can obey God and do what He calls you to do—whether you feel you have the ability to do the job or not. Sickness and weakness—those things we think God cannot use—are many times the exact things God uses to glorify His name."[3]

Perfecting Strength

1. a. The apostle Paul wrote to the Corinthian church, "If I must boast, I would rather boast about the things that show how weak I am" (2 Corinthians 11:30). Paul could speak from experience for he knew firsthand the value of weaknesses.

Read 2 Corinthians 12:1-10. What was the process by which Paul turned from relying on his own strength to relying on God's strength?

1664

b. Because Paul experienced the strength of God's grace, he would agree with Jeremiah: "But the LORD stands beside me like a great warrior" (Jeremiah 20:11). As you look up the following verses, write down Paul's experience of God standing beside him and strengthening him.

1657 2 Corinthians 4:7-10

1716 2 Timothy 4:16-18

c. God answered Paul's plea for the removal of the thorn by saying, "My grace is all you need. My power works best in weakness" (2 Corinthians 12:9). Why do you think that God's power works *best* in weakness?

1664

God's power neither displaces weakness nor overcomes it. On the contrary, it comes to its full strength *in* it (*en-astheneia*) [in weakness]. . . . Paul not only has accepted his weaknesses and learned to live with them, but he also takes pleasure in them. Why? Because these very weaknesses afford the opportunity for the power of Christ to rest on him. The verb *episkenoo* [dwell in], found only here in the New Testament, actually means to "make one's quarters in" or "take up one's abode in." So God's power not merely "rested on" or "over" Paul but took up residence in him.[4]

2. Embracing the truth that God's strength can be ideally experienced in our weakness can be challenging. Recount a time of weakness or vulnerability in your life when you were able to make similar declarations of God's grace and strength, or share a time when you observed this truth in another's life.

Indwelling Strength

3. The Amplified Bible translates 2 Corinthians 12:9 as "Therefore, I will all the more gladly glory in my weaknesses and infirmities, that the strength and power of Christ (the Messiah) may rest

(yes, may pitch a tent over and dwell) upon me!" Paul's desire was for the church to experience this indwelling. Read Ephesians 3:14-21 and write down Paul's intercession on our behalf.

Prayed he would strengthen with power
That Christ may dwell in our hearts
Grasp depth of His love

---

4. The psalmist Asaph and the prophet Isaiah wrote special truths to strengthen our faith. As you read these passages, what encouragement do you receive concerning God's strength?

Psalm 73:25-26

Isaiah 40:25-31

Hope in the Lord will renew strength
40:31

Concerning God's enabling power given in Isaiah 40:31, Russell Kelfer wrote, "How can that be? It is called grace. It is God waiting to do supernaturally what you cannot do naturally. You have two choices: You can chafe at your weakness and cry out to be delivered, or you can quietly submit to the Master Artist as He paints on the canvas of your life a brand-new, much deeper image of Himself."[5]

5. Paul begged the Lord three times to remove his thorn, and three times he was denied his request and was left with his weakness. Read 2 Corinthians 12:8-10 again and write down why you think Paul could "take pleasure" and "delight" (NIV) in his weaknesses. How does his response encourage you to boast about your weaknesses?

1664

> The literal translation of [2 Corinthians 12:10] adds a startling emphasis to it, allowing it to speak for itself with power we have probably never realized. It is as follows: "Therefore I take pleasure in being without strength, being insulted, experiencing emergencies, and being chased and forced into a corner for Christ's sake; for when I am without strength, I am *dynamite*."[6]
>
> *A. B. Simpson*

Thoughts from an Older Woman

No one knows exactly what Paul's thorn in the flesh really was. This in itself shows God's wisdom in the Scriptures. If the thorn were identified, then we could not universally apply the penetrating truth found in his experience. Thorns can take countless forms: physical, emotional, or even relational. No matter the cause, shape, or intensity, the universal remedy and the blessed comfort for each one is the sufficiency of God's grace.

"Whatever the *skolops* (thorn) was, the net effect for Paul was torment. The Greek term (*kolaphizw*) [torment] actually means to *'strike with the fist,' 'beat'* or *'cuff.'* The present tense suggests frequent bouts. Paul's stake was not an isolated episode. It repeatedly came back to plague him — like the school bully who waits each day for his victim to round the corner."[7] As much as Paul wanted this "splinter" (AMP) removed, he was able to understand and then to rejoice in God's beneficial purpose. This was a hand-picked agitation specifically sent by God to keep Paul from becoming proud.

Herein is our comfort: God's purpose is to conform us to the image of Christ (see Romans 8:29) and often He uses thorns to do so, but accompanying His purpose is His amazing grace and empowerment. God is a great Giver of strength, for when we are without strength, we are dynamite.

I experienced God's power in a special way when I was scheduled to tape a DVD series to complement one of my Bible studies. Although I enjoy speaking, I was fairly apprehensive about recording all eleven sessions in two days — a daunting task for an older woman like me! A few days before the taping, I experienced a wrenching bout of food poisoning; I was dealing with an ongoing infection; and the day before the recording I had to make an emergency visit to the dentist. Although I had a long list of things to remember to bring and do, I was blessed and grateful to have several friends come alongside to help.

My main concerns were my notes, looking presentable (a formidable task), and providing for the video director who was staying as a guest in our home.

This project was quickly becoming overwhelming, and I was definitely moving out of my comfort zone. I not only needed strength to tend to all the details, but strength to take me through the two days of teaching. But the reality was that I was coping with unexpected weaknesses; I was not at full capacity.

So, like Paul, I entreated the Lord: "Father, here I am. I am more than conscious of my weaknesses even when all my ducks are in a row, but now I feel helpless."

The Lord said to me, "My grace (My favor and loving-kindness and mercy) is enough for you . . . for My strength and power are made perfect (fulfilled and completed) and show themselves most effective in [your] weakness" (2 Corinthians 12:9, AMP).

And it was.

REFLECTION
Strengthened Through His Spirit to Glory in Weakness

Doug Nichols' life illustrates in an astounding way how God's favor, loving-kindness, and mercy are enough and how God can use our weakness for His purposes. Doug literally could experience the Master Artist painting on the canvas of his life a brand-new, much deeper image of Himself and for this he could glory in his infirmity. (At this time, the Lord is still using Doug.)

This is a compelling truth to comprehend: *God's power works best in my weakness.* I would like to encourage you to take some time alone and begin to absorb Paul's statement "When I am weak, then I am strong." Meditate on the implications of taking pleasure and even choosing to glory in your weaknesses.

One of our key verses is Philippians 4:13: "For I can do everything through Christ, who gives me strength." Before Paul wrote these words, he asked the Philippians to "keep putting into practice all you learned and received from me — everything you heard from me and saw me doing. Then the God of peace will be with you" (Philippians 4:9). After contemplating the Scriptures in this chapter, write in your journal the ways you can begin to put into practice what you have learned. Consider the following questions:

- How can the Scriptures and truths in this chapter change my perspective on my circumstances and my abilities?
- How can Paul's example and testimony free me from trying to summon my own strength to overcome my weaknesses and hardships?

Write a prayer expressing your desire to learn how to glory in your weaknesses so that the power of Christ can work through you.

PRAYER THOUGHT

Okay, Lord, I can do this: Empowered by Your Spirit, I will take pleasure in my weaknesses, for I can do everything through Christ, who gives me strength.

We have no power from God unless
We live in the persuasion that we
Have none of our own.[8]

John Owen

Thus I was strengthened according to the hand of the LORD my God upon me.

Ezra 7:28, NASB

SUGGESTED SCRIPTURE MEMORY: 2 Corinthians 12:9

CHAPTER THREE

Strong Enough to Be Teachable

But true wisdom and power are found in God; counsel and understanding are his.

JOB 12:13

It is impossible to doubt that guidance is a reality intended for, and promised to, every child of God. Christians who miss it thereby show only that they did not seek it as they should. It is right therefore to be concerned about one's own receptiveness to guidance, to study how to seek it.[1]

J. I. PACKER

William Wilberforce — A Man Who Had a Teachable Spirit

For forty-six years British politician William Wilberforce worked tirelessly to abolish the slave trade and ultimately slavery itself in Britain. Born in 1759 into an established and highly respected family, Wilberforce was gifted socially, enjoyed giving great parties, and loved to interact with people. When on his own for the first time in Cambridge, he began to adapt to the culture of the young men around him. A biographer observed, "Instead of getting or seeking good advice and counsel, he was using his wealth to grease the skids toward social prominence. There was a real possibility of his taking the wrong fork in the road and wasting his life — becoming an indolent, self-absorbed person."[2]

At about age twenty-five, though, Wilberforce underwent an evangelical conversion, which he viewed as the supreme event in his life. Finding Christ radically changed and transformed him to the extent that Wilberforce began to spend hours daily in earnest study of the Scriptures. He wrote to his sister, "Watch and pray, read the word of God, imploring that true wisdom which may enable you to comprehend and fix it in your heart, that it may gradually produce its effect under the operation of the Holy Spirit."[3]

Already a member of Parliament, he wondered if he should continue in public life, for at that time religious enthusiasm was generally regarded as a social transgression. Wilberforce wisely sought counsel from his mentor John Newton, Anglican clergyman and author of "Amazing Grace." One biographer noted, "Wilberforce's decision to confide in Newton could not have been better made. The former slave ship captain had a calm judgment that had matured through life experiences. . . . Newton showed great wisdom and helped Wilberforce resolve his misgivings about the reactions of friends to the renewal of his former religious convictions. He had need of such counsel, for he had been urged by at least one friend to retire from Parliament."[4]

Wilberforce was a prodigious reader, not only of the Word but of classic books. Despite his knowledge and position, he remained humble and teachable. A friend, Joseph Brown, had related this incident: "One day in conversation, Wilberforce gave him some advice. Brown expressed his thanks and said how much he should feel indebted, if, in conversation or correspondence, Wilberforce would at all times be his counselor, and, if necessary, correct him and point out all his faults. Wilberforce suddenly stopped, for they had been walking together, and replied, 'I will — but you must promise me one thing.' 'With pleasure,' Brown answered, little thinking what it was. 'Well, then,' continued

Wilberforce, 'in all your conversations and correspondence with me, be candid and open, and point out all my faults.'"[5]

Seeking God's Wisdom

1. a. Wilberforce actively sought wisdom and counsel. Wisdom is good sense and judgment, skill in living. True wisdom and power are found in God. Our Lord invites us, "Come and listen to my counsel. I'll share my heart with you and make you wise" (Proverbs 1:23). How does Proverbs 2:1-11 instruct us to seek wisdom, and what are the benefits when we do?

listen
search
1. gain knowledge of God.
2. Understanding
3 Wisdom

   b. It is right to be concerned about our receptivity to guidance. What can be learned from these Scriptures about seeking wisdom and discerning true wisdom?

   Proverbs 11:2 *Pride leads to disgrace but w/ humility comes wisdom*

   1 Corinthians 3:18 *Stop deceiving yourself. If you think you are wise by this worlds standards, you need to become a fool to be truly wise*

   James 3:13-17 *Live an honorable life, doing good works. Those who are peacemakers will plant seeds of peace & reap a harvest of righteousness.*

2. a. Because God is our source of wisdom, we need to be aware of how He guides us. As you study the verses below, recount the different ways God imparts His wisdom.

Psalm 37:30-31

30 *The godly offer good counsel - teach right from wrong.*
31. *They have made God's law their own*

Psalm 51:6

you desire honesty from the womb teaching me wisdom even there.

Psalm 119:105

Your word is a lamp to guide my feet & a light for my path

Acts 20:22-23

Holy Spirit guides so we need to trust.

No other person can speak to us from the bottom of our own hearts as the Holy Spirit does. . . . All of us must discover what it means to have no other comfort except the comfort that we ourselves can draw from our God in the lonely privacy of our own prayers. . . . Of course we have a need for teachers too, and for spiritual directors. But the even greater need is for every individual to cultivate a deep life of personal prayer and to hear and to heed the voice of the Lord. We need to take our problems to God first, before rushing out to spill them to others.[6]

Mike Mason

b. Proverbs 3:5-6 in *The Message* says, "Listen for GOD's voice in everything you do, everywhere you go; he's the one who will keep you on track." Of all the ways God speaks to you, which one do you respond to most readily? Why?

If I am in the habit of steadily facing myself with God, my conscience will always introduce God's perfect law and indicate what I should do. The point is will I obey? . . . The one thing that keeps the conscience sensitive to Him is the continual habit of being open to God on the inside. . . . When there is any debate, quit. "Why shouldn't I do this?" You are on the wrong track. There is no debate possible when conscience speaks.[7]

Oswald Chambers

c. Here is Oswald Chambers' definition of conscience: "Conscience is that faculty in me which attaches itself to the highest that I know and tells me what the highest I know demands that I do."[8] It is necessary, then, to have "the continual habit of being open to God on the inside." What do you think it means to be "open to God on the inside"? What would this openness look like in a life that is teachable?

Discerning God's Wisdom Through Others

3. a. Proverbs 12:15 tells us, "Fools think their own way is right, but the wise listen to others." Proverbs 15:22 teaches, "Plans go wrong for lack of advice; many advisers bring success." What characteristics of a godly counselor do you find in these passages?

Psalm 37:30-31

Proverbs 10:14

wise people treasure knowledge but a babbling fool invites disaster

Proverbs 14:16

Wise are cautious & avoid danger fools plunge ahead w/ reckless confidence

Proverbs 15:28

The heart of the godly thinks carefully before speaking; The mouth of the wicked overflows with evil words

b. Proverbs 28:23 states, "In the end, people appreciate honest criticism far more than flattery." In our conversations with godly mentors and friends, we sometimes hear words of correction. What can you learn from these passages about the value of instruction or reproof?

Proverbs 13:18

If you ignore criticism you will end up in poverty & disgrace. if you accept correction you will be honored.

Proverbs 15:31-32 *If you listen to constructive crit. you will be at home among the wise. If you reject discipline you harm yourself. If you listen you grow in understanding*

Proverbs 27:5-6 *Open rebuke is better than hidden love. Wounds from a sincere friend are better than kisses from an enemy*

c. Dawson Trotman made the following statement: "There is a kernel of truth in every criticism. Look for it, and when you find it, rejoice in its value."[9] What is your response to this statement: agree, disagree? Explain your thoughts.

The book of Proverbs teaches that many counselors are good because they provide safety and improve our odds of success (Proverbs 15:22). The book of Job shows that counselors can also mislead, even when their theology is orthodox. . . . They ignored Job's faithful pattern of life, focused on his torment, and concluded that he was reaping the effects of sin. God eventually called these counselors liars, reminding us that even the most orthodox theology must be rightly applied in order to please God and build up others. . . . While it is good to weigh advice from various sources, we must compare the counsel of others with what we believe to be right before God. . . . God might use human counselors to help us define his will, but God himself guides us.[10]

4. We find this thought in Proverbs 2:12: "Wisdom will save you from evil people, from those whose words are twisted." When people give advice, we need wisdom; we need to "compare the counsel of others with what we believe to be right before God." Write down how these passages exemplify the importance of discernment.

1 Samuel 24:1-7 *David / Saul in cave*

cut off robe.

2 Chronicles 24:17-19

5. Inherent in being teachable is a willingness to obey the godly counsel you have sought and been given. Jeremiah 42:1–43:4 gives an outstanding story about seeking and receiving God-given counsel. Jerusalem had just fallen to the Babylonians and the majority of the people were exiled, but a remnant was left in Judah. Jeremiah was God's anointed prophet, and he stayed with those who remained. Read this passage in Jeremiah, and consider what was at the heart of the remnant's disobedience. What speaks to you personally in this passage?

Thoughts from an Older Woman

Teachability is yielding to godly supervision and direction; it is having a willing spirit to learn; it is acknowledging that we cannot rely on our own insight. Being teachable does not come naturally to our prideful nature; that is why I think we need God's strength to be open to counsel.

Of all the ways of being taught, I prefer to learn from God's Word and the prompting of His Holy Spirit. Although I am not a fan of receiving correction, over the years I have learned that Proverbs 25:12 is true: "To one who listens, valid criticism is like a gold earring or other gold jewelry."

So when I am corrected, I go to the Lord and ask Him if there is a kernel of truth in what was said. I do want to know if I'm off track or need to change in any way. Once, after I had spoken at a seminar, a dear lady told me she had found fault with something I taught. I was distressed to be criticized, but I graciously thanked her, and as soon as I could, I earnestly prayed, "Lord, did You send this lady? Is there truth in what she said?" The Lord pointed out a kernel of truth — I did need to clarify a particular teaching, so I was able to accept her comment as if it were a gold earring. On occasion the Lord has answered that the criticism was not from Him and was not valid. When this happens, He reminds me that His grace is sufficient.

We studied how important it is to have discernment when counsel is given. I want to add an additional thought. There may be times when seeking guidance that what we sense from the Lord and what we hear from others may not agree. Paul was in this situation. We read in Acts 20:23 that the Holy Spirit told Paul about the suffering he would experience in Jerusalem. In Acts 21 we find the account of Paul receiving this counsel in Tyre: "These believers prophesied through the Holy Spirit that Paul should not go on to Jerusalem" (verse 4). One commentator observed this about the prophets in Tyre: "The Holy Spirit revealed to them, as he did to many others, that bonds and affliction awaited

St. Paul at Jerusalem. The inference that he should not go to Jerusalem was their own."[11] Their counsel was based on affection just as Peter's was when he reprimanded the Lord Jesus for saying He was to be killed. Jesus told Peter, "You are seeing things merely from a human point of view, not from God's" (Matthew 16:23). Just as Jesus knew that His mission was to go to the cross, Paul also knew that his mission was to obey the Lord for he was "bound by the Spirit to go to Jerusalem" (Acts 20:22).

When listening to counsel, it is necessary to "compare the counsel of others with what we believe to be right before God." So even godly counsel needs to be taken to the Lord. Chambers is right: "If I am in the habit of steadily facing myself with God, my conscience will always introduce God's perfect law and indicate what I should do." When we are teachable and desire only the Lord's will, then He will not let us be led astray. God will either confirm or cast doubt on any human counsel we receive. The book of James tells us, "If you need wisdom, ask our generous God, and he will give it to you. He will not rebuke you for asking" (James 1:5). Our part is to be open on the inside so that we allow God to have the final word, and then be willing to obey what He tells us.

> Every life that desires to be strong
> must have its "Most Holy Place"
> into which only God enters.[12]
>
> *Anonymous*

REFLECTION
Strengthened Through His Spirit to Be Teachable

Although William Wilberforce was a powerful man, he was sincerely teachable. God was able to strengthen him and use him in a mighty way because of his humility and openness.

After reflecting over this chapter and seeking the Lord's wisdom, prayerfully examine your own teachability. Ask the Lord to point out any willfulness in your spirit. Ask to be shown any barriers you erect in order to shield yourself from correction. Seeking counsel from an older woman and reading books by notable Christians are good ways of learning to be teachable.

Above all, get into the habit of steadily facing yourself with God by consistently reading His Word and being still before Him so that you can hear His voice. As Mike Mason wrote, "The even greater need is for every individual to cultivate a deep life of personal prayer and to hear and to heed the voice of the Lord."

Use your journal to write down what you hear from the Lord and perhaps from others who love you and love God. Write a prayer expressing your desire to be teachable in order to receive the counsel and strength that only the great Giver of strength can give.

 PRAYER THOUGHT

Okay, Lord, I can do this: Empowered by Your Spirit, I will be receptive to godly counsel and Your guidance, for I can do everything through Christ, who gives me strength.

 Be energetic in your life of salvation, reverent and sensitive before God. That energy is *God's* energy, an energy deep within you, God himself willing and working at what will give him the most pleasure.

Philippians 2:13, MSG

SUGGESTED SCRIPTURE MEMORY: Job 12:13

But true wisdom & power are found in God: Counsel & understanding are his.

CHAPTER FOUR

Strong Enough to Wait

Wait on the LORD;
Be of good courage,
And He shall strengthen your heart;
Wait, I say, on the LORD!

PSALM 27:14, NKJV

*Once we learn to wait for the Lord's leading in everything, we
will know the strength that finds its highest point in an even and
steady walk. Many of us are lacking the strength we so desire, but
God gives complete power for every task He calls us to perform.
Waiting — keeping yourself faithful to His leading — this is the
secret of strength.*[1]

SAMUEL DICKEY GORDON

Lorraine Scoble — Strength Found While Waiting

When a friend heard that I was writing a chapter on waiting, she
recommended that I contact her friend Lorraine. I did, and Lorraine
graciously shared her journey of waiting on God.

Lorraine met the Lord at age twenty-three and decided that she
needed undistracted time to focus solely on God. In order to do that,

she vowed not to date for a year. After the year was over she spent a summer in East Africa and was in her words, "Totally hooked. I remember praying on the flight home, thanking God and praising Him for such an amazing experience and telling Him that as soon as I was married, I would be ready to go back. It was almost as if I heard Him say, 'Why would you wait until you are married?' I knew in an instant that I needed to let go of my expectation and to trust the Lord for whatever He had in mind for me."

Over the next few years, she worked with international students and was preparing for a career overseas. But as she moved into her thirties Lorraine's feelings about being single hit hard. She pleaded with the Lord to take away her longing for a husband. Although she experienced many blessings and opportunities afforded more easily to a single woman, she still desired to be married.

On her way as a missionary to the Middle East, Lorraine discovered a poem by Martha Snell Nicholson titled "The Thorn" (see page 49). God used the poem to show her a new way of thinking about this "gift" of singleness. She realized that she could "offer this God-given longing back to Him, and count on Him to redeem it for His glory and my good, knowing that His grace is sufficient."

God also used Lorraine in the lives of many other single women as a witness to His faithfulness and tenderness in regard to their desires. During this season of her life, Lorraine experienced times of testing, loneliness, even depression. She described this period as having "sought and even fought to keep on trusting Him for His provision and entrusting Him with my heart's desires. He had never failed to provide for my needs, though not always in the way I would have chosen."

For twenty-two years as a missionary in the Middle East, Lorraine never believed that God was obligated to meet all her desires this side of heaven. She did not believe that she had been granted some special gift for relishing the single life, but she did believe that God lovingly chose this path for her and therefore it was good. She had come to look forward to her "marriage" in heaven and was settled in her heart that God planned for her to remain single.

But in 2010, Lorraine's heart was again strengthened in a very surprising way. Here are her words: "Imagine my astonishment and delight when a wonderful, godly man (serving in the same country, also having trusted God for years with his unfulfilled desire for a wife) asked me to consider marriage! God has now called us to a whole new world of trusting Him. We are awestruck and humbled by this gracious and unexpected gift, but mindful that this gift, too, is a temporary blessing, designed to point us to His ultimate reality. . . . I can't describe how sweet it is to contemplate together God's perfect timing, and to rejoice in His perfect ways. We would not trade a single moment of the 'waiting' and can only look back, as we look forward, with gratitude and wonder at the loving-kindness of our God."[2]

The Thorn

I stood a mendicant of God before His royal throne
And begged Him for one priceless gift that I could call my
    own.
I took the gift from out His hand, but as I would depart
I cried, "But Lord, this is a thorn! And it has pierced my
    heart."
He said, "My child, I give good gifts and gave My best to
    thee."
I took it home, and though at first the cruel thorn hurt sore,
As long years passed I learned at last to love it more and
    more.
I learned He never gives a thorn without this added grace:
He takes the thorn to pin aside the veil that hides His face.[3]

—*Martha Snell Nicholson*

Waiting *for* God

1. Lorraine rejoiced in God's perfect ways and found strength through every moment of waiting. Her willingness to wait and to trust God with her desires is inspiring. How do these verses inspire you and confirm your own journey of waiting?

   Psalm 37:5-7

   789

   Psalm 40:1-3

   793

   Isaiah 64:4

   1074

2. Someone humorously commented that "patience is a virtue that carries a lot of wait!" Using a dictionary or thesaurus, look up the meaning of "wait," and then based on what it means, write down one of your memorable experiences of waiting.

   To stay or rest in expectation

Waiting is nothing else but hope and trust lengthened.[4]

John Trapp

3. Hudson Taylor observed, "Quiet waiting before God would save from many a mistake and from many a sorrow."[5] What do these passages teach about the consequences of not waiting?

1 Samuel 13:5-14

390 you can loose, "big time"

Isaiah 30:15-17

1021

Dute 32:30

> When God brings a blank space, see that you do not fill it in, but wait.[6]
>
> *Oswald Chambers*

4. A godly saint commented, "When we wait *for* God, we are waiting until He is ready."[7] Read about some of the stalwarts of the faith who waited until God was ready. What blessings did they receive?

Luke 2:21-32

1473 Simeon was promised he would not die before he saw the Messiah

Hebrews 6:13-15

1730 Abraham recieved what was promised

5. Beyond waiting for God to do something for us that we want, Scripture does mention other aspects of waiting for God. For what do these verses specifically direct us to wait?

928 Proverbs 20:22 *Do not say I'll pay you back for this wrong. Wait for the Lord & he will deliver you.*

1619 Romans 8:18-25

1672 Galatians 5:5 *But by faith we eagerly await through the Spirit the righteousness for which we hope.*

Waiting *upon* God

6. Hope, trust, patience, and expectancy are essential aspects of waiting. In these Scriptures, what choices were made and blessings bestowed in waiting upon God?

761 Psalm 5:1-3 *David chose to pray & he was heard.*

812 Psalm 62:5-8

102 | Isaiah 30:18

133 | Micah 7:7

Watch in hope my God will hear me

A soul cannot seek close fellowship with God, or attain the abiding consciousness of waiting on Him all day long, without a completely honest and entire surrender to all His will. . . . We are still very slow to learn that this waiting must and can be the very breath of our life, a continuous resting in God's presence and His love, a constant yielding of ourselves for Him to perfect His work in us. Let us once again listen and meditate until our heart says with new conviction: *"Blessed are they that wait for him."*[8]

Andrew Murray

---

7. Gordon's thought on waiting — "keeping yourself faithful to His leading" — gives a spiritual perspective. From what you have learned so far, write a biblical summary of what it means to wait.

God, the one and only—
> I'll wait as long as he says.
> Everything I need comes from him,
> > so why not?
> He's solid rock under my feet,
> > breathing room for my soul,
> An impregnable castle:
> > I'm set for life.

Psalm 62:1-2, MSG.

---

8. a. Andrew Murray stated that "God [is] altogether most worthy of being waited on."[9] As we rest and trust our most worthy God, what can we be doing as we wait?

791 Psalm 37:34

Wait & keep his way
Put your hope in the Lord
Travel steadily along his path.

909 Proverbs 8:24-35

look
for whoever finds me finds life
& receives favor

1758 2 Peter 3:8-14

Make every effort to be found
living peaceful lives — pure & blameless
in his sight

b. When asked why he was frustrated and irritable, Phillips Brooks, a British pastor, voiced the heart of us all: "The trouble is that I'm in a hurry and God is not."[10] As you look back over this chapter, write down any encouragement or insight you have received to keep you from being disheartened while you wait patiently and expectantly for and upon the Lord.

> Don't steal tomorrow from God's hands. Give Him time to speak to you and reveal His will. He is never late — learn to wait.[11]

Thoughts from an Older Woman

In the 1970s my family made a major move so that Jack could receive training with a ministry. In our previous location, I had led Bible studies in my home, but it became very clear to me from the Lord that with this move I was not to be involved in ministry to women. During this three-year period I learned to wait consistently *upon* the Lord. I memorized Scripture. I met with a mentor. I learned in a very practical way to live my priorities. I discovered that the Lord had not forgotten me or put me aside but was deepening my intimacy with Him and fine-tuning my faith. It was a precious time of waiting *upon* the Lord which, over the years, has ultimately strengthened me to wait *for* the Lord.

Andrew Murray wrote that waiting upon the Lord is being continually conscious of His company. It is desiring His companionship to the extent that we spend time with Him by being still and listening to His voice, especially through His Word. Having this time of waiting upon the Lord taught me that, in a sense, I am on the Lord's "wait staff." I exist to serve the Lord, to wait on His bidding. My time is His, and I am to be available to attend to His commands and direction or to be still if He so chooses. Part of the definition of *wait* is having a sense of readiness to act when called upon. As I wait upon the Lord, *keeping myself faithful to His leading,* then He is able to teach me lessons that can be learned only in His "waiting room."

I will never forget the day the Lord "lifted the cloud" (as He did with the Israelites in the wilderness) and led me slowly back into ministry with women. Now, though, my strength was renewed. Now I knew that God and my family were my priorities. Now I knew that apart from Christ I could do nothing, yet with Him I could do all things. My time of waiting gave me the needed security of knowing that whenever the Lord wanted me to wait in the future, I would not miss out on what He had for me. What I learned was that the Lord was using this time to strengthen me. As Charles Spurgeon wrote, "You have no reserve of strength. Every day you must seek help from above. It is a blessed assurance to know that your daily ration of renewed strength is provided through ongoing meditation, prayer, and waiting on God."[12]

One reason it is hard for us to be still is that we live in a fast-paced society, yet I am amazed at how willing we are to wait for something that is temporal. I have a friend who waited more than three hours to have her book signed by a former president. We read about and see pictures of people waiting in line for hours and even longer to get concert tickets or a new electronic device. Can we not have this same zeal to wait for God who is "altogether most worthy of being waited on"?

Once I ordered a special book for a friend. When I received it, I wrote a note inside the cover and looked forward to giving it to her. As I entered her home, I saw that she already had the same book on her coffee table. As I gave her my book, she sighed and said, "Oh, I wish I had waited!" She had just purchased her copy the day before.

It is not wrong to get things we want, but I wonder if this might be the way God feels when He wants to give us a gift but we are unwilling to wait. How many times do we run ahead of God? How many times has He had a "book" He wanted to present to us with this inscription: "I've been waiting for the right time to give this to you. Here it is, given in love with My name on it." Again Spurgeon reminds us, "The greatest danger is that we would become impatient and miss the blessing."[13]

Life is full of waiting—waiting to marry, waiting to have or adopt children, waiting for a loved one to know Christ, waiting for healing, waiting for a job, waiting for circumstances to improve, waiting to "see the goodness of the LORD in the land of the living" (Psalm 27:13, NIV). Because waiting is something we often must contend with, let's embrace this teaching of waiting and all of its ramifications in order to experience the fresh strength that God alone can bestow. Samuel Dickey Gordon also observed, "It is always safe to trust God's methods and to live by His clock."[14]

> But those who wait upon GOD get fresh strength.
> They spread their wings and soar like eagles,
> They run and don't get tired,
> they walk and don't lag behind.
>
> *Isaiah 40:31, MSG*

REFLECTION
Strengthened Through His Spirit to Wait

Peter Marshall prayed, "Teach us, Lord, the disciplines of patience, for to wait is often harder than to work."[15] How very true! In our "get it done" world it is incredibly hard to remain inactive, to just rest and rely on the Lord. Lorraine came to a point in her life where she acknowledged that the path He had for her was good. She did not try to manipulate circumstances (like move to a country with more eligible men) or run ahead of God by marrying just for the sake of getting married. She was patient, she trusted, and she waited upon God with the gift of her thorn.

Read through the poem "The Thorn" again. Do you have a particular thorn that you are waiting to have removed? What does your life look like as you are waiting? Are you waiting *upon* God as you are waiting *for* God? Are you able to be completely honest and entirely surrender to His will? Are you willing to wait for the Lord to settle a matter or give you further insight where you have been wronged? George Matheson once said, "My dear God, I have never thanked You for my thorns. I have thanked You a thousand times for my roses but not once for my thorns."[16]

Be still before the Lord, ask Him these questions, and wait in silence until you sense that He is your refuge, a rock where no enemy can reach you. In your journal, record your answers to the questions and any thoughts you hear from the Lord.

Consider this prayer: "Lord, 'Not my will, but Yours be done' [Luke 22:42]. I do not know what to do, and I am in great need. But I will wait until You divide the flood before me or drive back my enemies. I will wait even if You keep me here many days, for my heart is fixed on You alone, dear Lord. And my spirit will wait for You with full confidence that You will still be my joy and my salvation, 'for you have been my refuge, [and] a strong tower against the foe' [Ps. 61:3]."[17]

 PRAYER THOUGHT

Okay, Lord, I can do this: Empowered by Your Spirit, I will wait with my heart fixed on You, for I can do everything through Christ, who gives me strength.

GOD takes the time to do everything right — everything.
Those who wait around for him are the lucky ones.
Isaiah 30:18, MSG

SUGGESTED SCRIPTURE MEMORY: Psalm 27:14

Wait for the Lord: Be strong & take heart & wait for the Lord.

CHAPTER FIVE

Strong Enough to Exercise Self-Control

> *Better to be patient than powerful; better to have self-control than to conquer a city.*
>
> Proverbs 16:32

> *The heathen type of heroism was strength of arm — bodily strength, manly courage against an outward foe. The spiritual and the Christian type is in strength of will against evil, self-mastery, self-conquest, sublime patience.*[1]
>
> E. Johnson

Carl — A Man Who Exercised Self-Control

Carl was a quiet man who would greet you with a big smile and a firm handshake. He was eighty-seven years old, and he had a slight limp from a bullet wound received in WWII. Carl lived for more than fifty years in a once-prosperous neighborhood that now increasingly experienced random violence, gangs, and drug activity.

When the local church asked for volunteers to care for the garden behind the minister's residence, Carl signed up. One day, just as he was finishing his watering, three gang members approached him. Ignoring their attempt to intimidate him, he simply asked, "Would you like a drink from the hose?" The tallest and toughest-looking said, "Yeah, sure." As Carl offered the hose to him, the other two threw Carl down on the ground and stole his retirement watch and wallet and ran.

The minister looked out of his window and saw the old man struggling to get up. He ran to help him, asking, "Are you okay? Are you hurt?" Stunned, Carl passed a hand over his brow and sighed, shaking his head, "Just some punk kids. I hope they'll wise up someday."

A few weeks later the three returned. Just as before their threat went unchallenged. Carl again offered them a drink from his hose. This time they didn't rob him, but wrenched the hose from his hand and drenched him head to foot. When they finished their humiliation, they sauntered off down the street, laughing and throwing catcalls and curses back to their victim. Carl just watched them, picked up his hose, and continued watering.

Toward the end of the summer Carl was doing some tilling and was startled by the sudden approach of someone behind him. He stumbled and fell and as he struggled to regain his footing, he saw the tall leader of his tormentors reaching his hand toward him. Carl braced himself for an attack.

"Don't worry, old man, I'm not gonna hurt you this time." The young man spoke softly, still offering the tattooed and scarred hand to Carl. After he helped Carl get up, he handed him a crumpled paper bag.

"What's this?" Carl asked.

"It's your stuff," the youth explained. "It's your stuff back. Even the money in your wallet."

"I don't understand," Carl said. "Why would you help me now?"

Embarrassed, the young man replied, "I learned something from you. I ran with that gang and hurt people; we picked you because you were old and we knew we could do it. But every time we came and did something to you, instead of yelling and fighting back, you tried to give us a drink. You didn't hate us for hating you. You kept showing love against our hate." He stopped for a moment. "I couldn't sleep after we stole your stuff, so here it is back." He paused. "That bag's my way of saying thanks for straightening me out, I guess."

And with that, he walked off down the street.[2]

The Necessity of Self-Control

1. It took strength for Carl not to react to the young men who accosted him. Self-control is the ability to exercise self-restraint over one's feelings and reactions. It is temperance, self-discipline, and self-mastery. What can you learn from these verses about the necessity of self-control?

Proverbs 16:32 *Better a patient man, than Warrior - a man who controls his temper than one who takes a city.*

Proverbs 25:28 *Like a city whose walls are broken down is a man who lacks self-control. Self control can be a protective "wall" to repel temptation*

1 Corinthians 9:24-27

the prize of salvation

2. Peter wrote to the church, "You are a slave to whatever controls you" (2 Peter 2:19). In showing our need for self-control, what specific areas of our lives do the following Scriptures address?

912   Proverbs 10:19 *When words are many, sin is not absent, but he who holds his tongue is wise.*

937   Proverbs 25:16 *If you find honey, eat just enough -- too much of it, and you will vomit.*

942   Proverbs 29:11,22 *"A fool gives full vent to his*
943   *anger, but a wise man keeps himself under control. 22. An angry man stirs up dissension & a hot tempered one commits many sins*

Galatians 5:19-21

1673

Concerning anger, Solomon wrote, "Do not hasten in your spirit to be angry, for anger rests in the bosom of fools" (Ecclesiastes 7:9, NKJV). J. Willcock observes in his commentary: "That anger is in some circumstances a lawful passion no reasonable person can deny; but the Preacher points out two forms of it that are in themselves evil. The first is when anger is 'hasty,' not calm and deliberate, as the lawful expression of moral indignation, but the outcome of wounded self-love; and the second when it is detained too long, when it 'rests' in the bosom. As a momentary, instinctive feeling excited by the sight of wickedness, it is lawful; but when it has a home in the heart it changes its character and becomes malignant hatred or settled scornfulness."[3]

3. Look again at Proverbs 25:28. *The Message* illustrates a lack of self-control in this way: "A person without self-control is like a house with its doors and windows knocked out." In what way would you describe or explain the repercussions of a lack of self-control?

The Source of Self-Control

4. "Self-control actually means taking responsibility to deal in a godly way with temptations, sinful desires and ungodly behaviour, whether in thought, word or deed."[4] We encounter myriad circumstances that test our ability to restrain ourselves. How is it possible to have the strength necessary to exercise self-control? Read these Scriptures and record your insights.

Romans 8:5-14

Galatians 5:22-26

2 Timothy 1:7 *For God did not give us a spirit of timidity, but a spirit of power of love and of self discipline*

What does Paul mean by self-control? His word *enkrateia* has a rich history in Greek philosophy. The root, *krat*, means power or control. *Enkrateia* means power over oneself in the sense of persistence, endurance or restraint, mastery of one's appetites and passions. For Paul, *enkrateia* ultimately is not an autonomous human achievement: *enkrateia* is a fruit of the Spirit, a supernatural byproduct of responding by faith to grace and walking by the Spirit, as we are led by the Spirit.[5]

Jack Wisdom

---

5. When we are controlled by the Spirit, we are able to choose to respond in a godly way. In what ways can these verses help you to exercise self-control?

920 Proverbs 15:28 *The heart of the righteous weighs its answers, but the mouth of the wicked gushes evil*

926 Proverbs 19:11 *A man's wisdom gives him patience; it is to his glory to overlook an offense.*

1616 Romans 6:12 *Therefore do not let sin reign in your mortal body so that you obey its evil desires.*

1742 James 1:19-25

When you are about to say something in conversation with others and you sense a gentle restraint from His quiet whisper, heed the restraint and refrain from speaking.[6]

---

6. "Self-control is the exercise of inner strength under the direction of sound judgment that enables us to do, think, and say the things that are pleasing to God."[7] As you consider this definition of *self-control* and the Scriptures you have studied, take time to examine your life and pinpoint the people or circumstances that tend to cause you to lose self-control. Fill in your answers in the columns below.

My unique challenges	My typical response	The Spirit-controlled response
Only Eating	I loose it I give in to tempt.	Prov. 19:11 Prov 25:28

There is a place of stillness that allows God the opportunity to work for us and gives us peace. It is a stillness that ceases our scheming, self-vindication, and the search for a temporary means to an end through our own wisdom and judgment. Instead, it lets God provide an answer, through His unfailing and faithful love, to the cruel blow we have suffered.

Oh, how often we thwart God's intervention on our behalf by taking up our own cause or by striking a blow in our defense! May God grant each of us this silent power and submissive spirit.[8]

A. B. Simpson

Thoughts from an Older Woman

To me, someone who lacks control is exposed, laid bare. Every time I speak hastily or respond contentiously, I feel that I have stepped onto a stage in front of a large audience dressed in a flimsy costume, shouting, "Look at how foolish I am!" Just recently during lunch at a conference, one woman at the table commented that she had wintered in Florida but someday would like to spend the winter in Arizona. I blurted out, "Oh, please come. I think you will really enjoy Arizona. It's nicer than Florida, mainly because we don't have mosquitoes or hurricanes!" As soon as those words left my mouth, I remembered that my hostess and her close friend, both seated next to me, had just bought condos in Naples, Florida. Notwithstanding my friends' presence, my comment was careless and inconsiderate. There I was out on the stage, parading around, exposed for my thoughtlessness. I did not think before I spoke. I did not allow the Holy Spirit to direct my thoughts. I did not exercise self-control.

In Philippians we are reminded that "God is working in you, giving you the desire and the power to do what pleases him" (2:13). God is indeed working, but He needs our cooperation and obedience to His promptings. The Lord gives His strength, but we must discipline ourselves to appropriate and to receive His power. That is why it is called *self*-control. God asks us to use the strength He imparts to master ourselves.

It is wonderfully freeing to understand that I am no longer controlled by my sinful nature. It does take the Lord's supernatural grace and strength, though, to think before I speak, to turn away from temptation, and to act in a godly manner in thought, word, or deed. If I rely on my own strength, it is almost impossible for me to be slow to anger or to deny my sinful desires. But if my mind is set on what the Spirit desires, if I am allowing the Spirit to empower me with His strength, then I can say, "Lord, in Your strength, I can do this." As I become Spirit-controlled, I become self-controlled, and I am enabled to respond in ways that please the Lord.

There is a delightful paragraph found in THE CHRONICLES OF NARNIA, by C. S. Lewis. In the chronicles he tells the story of four children who visit a mythical kingdom where he portrays the Lord as a lion named Aslan. Lucy, the youngest, had been misunderstood by her family, and Susan was making deprecating remarks about her such as, "What if I behaved liked Lucy?" As they began their trek across a mountain, Lewis wrote, "Lucy went first, biting her lip and trying not to say all the things she thought of saying to Susan. But she forgot them when she fixed her eyes on Aslan."[9]

> May God grant us more of the Spirit of Christ, who "when they hurled their insults at him . . . did not retaliate. . . . Instead, he entrusted himself to him who judges justly" (1 Peter 2:23).[10]
>
> *A. B. Simpson*

REFLECTION
Strengthened Through His Spirit to Exercise Self-Control

I've tried to put myself in Carl's place. I've thought that perhaps he should have done something to protect himself. But as I have considered his particular circumstances, I believe that even if he had tried to defend himself, there is no predicting how the young men might have reacted. He was outnumbered in this attack, and even as a seasoned war veteran, he chose not to fight back. In Carl's exercise of self-control, God used him to reach the leader of the gang, who eventually became a Christian and named his own son after Carl.

Self-control is double-edged — it ultimately has an impact on others and it blesses you because you have borne the fruit of the Spirit. In order to conserve this fruit, choose some key Scriptures from this chapter, record them in your journal, and begin to memorize them and pray them into your life. Ask God to show you where you are most vulnerable and what tends to trigger your lack of self-control. Find a place of stillness where God can work and give you peace. Listen for His answers whenever you are tempted to react according to your sinful nature. Purpose to pray before you make a hasty response or act impulsively. Pray for the spiritual strength of self-mastery, self-conquest, and sublime patience. Pray as David did, "May the words of my mouth and the meditation of my heart be pleasing to you, O LORD, my rock and my redeemer" (Psalm 19:14).

 PRAYER THOUGHT

Okay, Lord, I can do this: Empowered by Your Spirit and fixing my eyes on You, I will exercise self-control because I can do everything through Christ, who gives me strength.

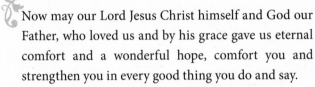

If you would learn self-mastery, begin by yielding yourself to the One Great Master.[11]

Johann Friedrich Lobstein

Now may our Lord Jesus Christ himself and God our Father, who loved us and by his grace gave us eternal comfort and a wonderful hope, comfort you and strengthen you in every good thing you do and say.

2 Thessalonians 2:16-17

SUGGESTED SCRIPTURE MEMORY: Proverbs 16:32

CHAPTER SIX

Strong Enough to Be Holy

May he strengthen your hearts so that you will be blameless and holy in the presence of our God and Father when our Lord Jesus comes with all his holy ones.

1 Thessalonians 3:13, NIV

No one overcomes the corruptions of his heart except by the enabling strength of the Spirit of God.[1]

Jerry Bridges

Suzanne — A Woman Who Learned "Never Compromise"

After the morning session of a conference where I spoke on choosing to be holy in today's world, "Suzanne" asked if we could talk privately. She began her story by saying that she had been a contented housewife with three children. After several years, Suzanne began to look for a job and learned that a man from her church needed a secretary. She was thrilled to go to work for him and enjoyed being in a small office. One day her boss suggested that they go to lunch. One lunch led to another, and before long they were having an affair. Suzanne was smitten, and in the heat of passion, she cast her husband aside in order to be free to remarry. Her boss, though, was unwilling to leave his wife and family. This left

Suzanne alone; reconciliation was an impossibility, for her husband had been deeply wounded by her unfaithfulness.

When we talked, it had been three years since her divorce. With tears and heartache, she related the pain she continues to experience in being single and seeing the repercussions her children must endure living in two different homes with parents who are no longer together. Her last words to me were, "Cynthia, please tell as many women as you can to never compromise; the consequences are too devastating."

God's Design to Be Holy

1. I'm sure that Suzanne would heartily agree that we cannot be reminded enough of God's longing for us to be holy. Paul wrote to the young disciple Timothy, "God saved us and called us to live a holy life" (2 Timothy 1:9). How do these verses confirm God's desire for our holiness?

   Ephesians 5:1-5

   1 Thessalonians 4:3-8

   1 Peter 1:13-16

   Be holy because I am holy

2. Oswald Chambers taught, "Redemption means that Jesus Christ can put into any man the hereditary disposition that was in Himself, and all the standards He gives are based on that disposition: *His teaching*

is for the life He puts in."[3] How do the following verses encourage you to trust in and to depend upon God for holiness?

1 Thessalonians 5:23-24

2 Thessalonians 3:3

2 Peter 1:3-4

Holiness is not a badge you wear, it is a privilege you bear. It is not a source of personal pride, but an invisible magnet drawing you to humble repentance and deep recognition of personal sin: not in others, but in yourself. . . . It will always be an unconscious outpouring of who He is, and the recognition will go to the One who sent His Holy Spirit to be Holy in us. One reason we do not understand holiness is that we do not understand grace. The ultimate degree to which holiness flows through your life will depend, not on your determination or your moral diligence, but on your willingness to yield to the nature of God in humble surrender. You possess no holiness apart from God.[2]

Russell Kelfer

3. Russell Kelfer described holiness as an invisible magnet drawing us to humble repentance and a deep recognition of personal sin. Using a dictionary and any of the earlier verses or quotations, write out your definition of what it means to be holy.

> If we are to make any progress in the pursuit of holiness, we must assume our responsibility to discipline or train ourselves. But we are to do all this in total dependence on the Holy Spirit to work in us and strengthen us with the strength that is in Christ.[4]
>
> *Jerry Bridges*

Our Responsibility to Be Holy

4. Jerry Bridges noted, "The death of Christ secured for us not only freedom from the penalty of sin, but also deliverance from the dominion of sin in our lives."[5] What do you learn from these verses about our role in putting to death the sinful nature?

Romans 6:11-14

Romans 12:1-2

1638 1 Corinthians 6:18-20

1669 Galatians 2:20

> The free committal of myself to God gives the Holy
> Spirit the chance to impart to me the holiness of Jesus
> Christ.[6]
>
> *Oswald Chambers*

---

5. In the book of James, we find that "temptation comes from our
   own desires, which entice us and drag us away" (1:14). What do
   these Scriptures teach us about specific actions we can take to overcome our sinful desires?

470 Psalm 119:11

1719 Titus 2:11-14

1738 Hebrews 12:1-4

1745 James 4:7

1754 1 Peter 5:8-9

The Holy Spirit cannot be located as a Guest in a house,
He invades everything. When once I decide that my
"old man" (i.e., the heredity of sin) should be identified
with the death of Jesus, then the Holy Spirit invades me.
He takes charge of everything, my part is to walk in the
light and to obey all that He reveals. When I have made
the moral decision about sin, it is easy to reckon actually
that I am dead unto sin, because I find the life of Jesus
there all the time.[7]

Oswald Chambers

God's Grace and Blessing to Those Who Are Holy

6. Although Suzanne still had to bear the consequences of her sin, she
   did repent, was forgiven, and was reconciled to God. How is God's
   grace expressed in these Scriptures?

1984 Psalm 32:1-5

Proverbs 28:13

1 John 1:8-9

---

7. Holiness in itself is a blessing, but the Lord also honors our purity. What do we gain when our lives are holy?

Psalm 15:1-2

Matthew 5:8

2 Timothy 2:20-21

---

8. Oswald Chambers wrote, "You no more need a holiday from spiritual concentration than your heart needs a holiday from beating. You cannot have a moral holiday and remain moral, nor can you have a spiritual holiday and remain spiritual. God wants you to be entirely His, and this means that you have to watch to keep yourself

fit."[8] Write a paragraph stating your desire to pursue holiness and how you plan to "watch to keep yourself fit."

Thoughts from an Older Woman

Living a holy life in today's world brings a multitude of challenges. Because our society is permeated with enticements to live according to the flesh, it is easy to be influenced and become conformed to our culture. Charles Spurgeon observed, "A Christian may grow callous so slowly that the sin which once startled no longer alarms. By degrees we become comfortable with sin."[9] One verse I have memorized is Psalm 141:4: "Don't let me drift toward evil or take part in acts of wickedness. Don't let me share in the delicacies of those who do wrong." I have hidden this verse in my heart because sometimes I find myself sharing in the "delicacies" of sin without being startled by them.

Because the desire of my heart is to refrain from doing anything that would grieve the Holy Spirit who lives within me, I have made some decisions, some ways to "watch," to keep me from becoming comfortable with sin. As my wise son-in-law, Mark Graper, profoundly commented, "The essence of self-discipline lies in making commitments in times of strength in order to avoid making decisions in times of weakness."

- I know that I must consistently spend time with the Lord daily. I believe Oswald Chambers is right: I can take no spiritual holiday. I also believe Jesus when He said, "Apart from me you can do nothing" (John 15:5). I read the Word, for it teaches, reproves, corrects, and trains me in righteousness (see 2 Timothy 3:16). I pray and listen. One of my prayers is that I will always be sensitive and obedient to the Holy Spirit when He convicts me of sin.

- I have purposed to be on guard in my relationships with men, physically and emotionally. Proverbs 4:23 says, "Guard your heart above all else, for it determines the course of your life."
- I carefully choose what I read, listen to, and watch. My one guideline is: "If I do this activity, will it please God?" A verse that helps me is, "I will lead a life of integrity in my own home" (Psalm 101:2).
- I memorize verses for my mind and tongue. Ephesians 4:29 says, "Do not let any unwholesome talk come out of your mouths, but only what is helpful for building others up according to their needs, that it may benefit those who listen" (NIV).
- I dress modestly because of 1 Timothy 2:9: "I want women to be modest in their appearance." Someone asked me one time to define *modest,* and this was my answer: "Everything that needs to be covered up is covered up and stays covered up."

As I end this chapter, I am again blessed to be reminded of God's great love, care, and grace toward us. He not only sent His Son to pay the penalty for our sins, He also gives us the strength to say no to sin. As Mike Mason noted, "Becoming a Christian does not eradicate the sinful nature; rather, it gives one a place to take a stand against it."[10] The wonder of God's grace is that the Holy Spirit lives within us to keep us on the right path, to check our sinfulness, and to empower us to make the right choices. How thankful I am that we have an "invasive" God who is faithful to strengthen us and guard us against the evil one; He only needs our humble dependence and willingness to yield to His leading. On our own we cannot be holy, but by His enabling strength we can.

"The faithful," wrote John Murray, "are not perfect in holiness. But they have been translated from the realm of sin and death to that of righteousness and life. Sin is now their burden and plague. Why? Because it is not their realm, they are not at home with it. It is foreign country to them. They are in the world, but not of it."[11]

REFLECTION
Strengthened Through His Spirit to Be Holy

God calls us, His children, to holiness because He Himself is holy. It is not easy to remember this when we are confronted with the "pleasures of sin." This was Suzanne's downfall. The enemy was looking for someone to devour and Suzanne was neither self-controlled nor alert. Her life is a testimony to what happens when we take a spiritual holiday. We are to be holy, and "His divine *power* has given us everything we need for life and godliness" (2 Peter 1:3, NIV, emphasis added), so we are essentially without an excuse.

As you spend time alone with the Lord, ask Him to expose any areas of vulnerability or any inclinations you have toward ungodliness. Write in your journal your commitments to keep yourself holy in order to avoid making wrong decisions in time of weakness. Pray that from this day forward you will yield in humble surrender to the Lord, walk obediently in His light, and appropriate the enabling strength of the Holy Spirit to live a pure and holy life.

 PRAYER THOUGHT

Okay, Lord, I can do this: Empowered by Your Spirit, I will freely commit myself to live a holy life, for I can do everything through Christ, who gives me strength.

Our sins twisted the crown of thorns; our sins drove the nails into his hands and feet; on account of our sins his blood was shed. Surely the thought of Christ crucified should make us loathe all sin.[12]

J. C. Ryle

As obedient children, let yourselves be pulled into a way of life shaped by God's life, a life energetic and blazing with holiness. God said, "I am holy; you be holy."

1 Peter 1:15-16, MSG

SUGGESTED SCRIPTURE MEMORY: 1 Thessalonians 3:13

CHAPTER SEVEN

Strong Enough for Spiritual Warfare

A final word: Be strong in the Lord and in his mighty power. Put on all of God's armor so that you will be able to stand firm against all strategies of the devil. . . . Pray in the Spirit at all times and on every occasion. Stay alert and be persistent in your prayers for all believers everywhere.

EPHESIANS 6:10-11,18

Prayer is the process of fellowshipping with God until your heart and His beat as one. It is not a casual experience; it is spiritual warfare.[1]

RUSSELL KELFER

Dwight L. Moody — A Recipient of Spiritual Warfare Through Prayer

D. L. Moody, founder of Moody Church and Moody Bible Institute, shared his experience of receiving powerful intercessory prayer with his close friend, R. A. Torrey. In his book *The Power of Prayer*, R. A. Torrey recorded Moody's story:

After the great Chicago fire in 1871, Moody made arrangements to feed the poor and to provide for the rebuilding of his church. He then left for England where he wanted to rest and be refreshed — particularly through the teaching of Charles Spurgeon, pastor of New Park Street Chapel in London, and George Mueller, evangelist and director of Ashley Down Orphanage. Although he did not intend to preach at all, he did accept an invitation from his friend, Mr. Lessey, to speak at the morning and evening services in his church north of London. But as he preached that morning, he said, "I had no power, no liberty; it seemed like pulling a heavy train up a steep grade, and as I preached I said to myself, 'What a fool I was to consent to preach. I came here to hear others, and here I am preaching.'"[2]

With a heavy heart Moody went to the evening service, but as he preached "it seemed as if the powers of an unseen world had fallen upon the audience. As I drew to the close of my sermon I got courage to draw the net. I asked all that would then and there accept Christ to rise, and about five hundred people arose to their feet. I thought there must be some mistake; so I asked them to sit down, and then I said, 'There will be an after-meeting in the vestry, and if any of you will really accept Christ meet the pastor and me in the vestry.'"[3]

Before Moody and Lessey left for the vestry, Moody repeated the invitation more clearly and they all arose for a second time; then he repeated it a third time and all the people stood again. He still thought that there was some misunderstanding and told the assembly, "I'm going to Ireland tomorrow, but your pastor will be here tomorrow night. If you really mean what you have said here tonight, meet him here." After Moody reached Ireland, he received a telegram from Pastor Lessey telling him that he needed to return because more people came out on Monday night and a revival had begun. Moody hurried back and held a series of meetings that added hundreds of people in North London to the body of Christ.

When Moody finished telling this story to his friend, Torrey responded, "Mr. Moody, someone must have been praying."

"Oh," he said, "did I not tell you that? That is the point of the whole story. There were two sisters in that church, one of whom was bedridden; the other one heard me that Sunday morning. She went home and said to her sister, 'Who do you suppose preached for us this morning? . . . Mr. Moody of Chicago.' No sooner had she said it than her sister turned pale as death and said, 'What! Mr. Moody of Chicago? I have read of him in an American paper and I have been praying God to send him to London, and to send him to our church. If I had known he was to preach this morning I would have eaten no breakfast, I would have spent the whole morning in fasting and prayer. Now, sister, go out, lock the door, do not let any one come to see me, do not let them send any dinner; I am going to spend the whole afternoon and evening in fasting and prayer.'"

Torrey adds, "And pray she did, and God heard and answered."[4]

Our Enemy

1. When D. L. Moody preached on Sunday morning, he described the struggle he had in preaching. This is one example of the ways our enemy, Satan, can oppose the truth. What else do these Scriptures tell you about Satan?

Ephesians 6:10-13

We need the "Armor of God" to stand up to the Devil.

1 Peter 5:8

(foot notes)

1 John 5:18-19

(foot notes)

1786 Revelation 12:7-12

> We must never underestimate the enemy. We must never forget the utter malice of his intentions, the ruthlessness of his assaults, the subtlety of his tactics. Yet, we need not walk in fear, for God has provided mighty weapons for our ultimate victory in spiritual warfare.[5]
>
> *Paul Thigpen*

---

2. In 1 John 3:8 we are told, "But the Son of God came to destroy the works of the devil." Christ's death on the cross rendered ineffective the works of Satan by freeing us from sin's power and giving us His power to stand firm against the enemy. What choices are you urged to make while living in Satan's territory?

1627 Romans 13:13-14

1679 Ephesians 4:21-24

1692 Colossians 3:5-11

1754
1 Peter 5:9

Resist

Using the imagery of clothing, Paul calls believers to put off the old, sinful life driven by the devil and to put on a new, pure life directed by the Holy Spirit. As they do so, they recognize their reliance on God's grace and power.[6]

---

3. Because we live in the world, we must contend with the strategies of the devil. How would you describe your own view of Satan's tactics?

He invades my mind. Puts thoughts in my head.

C. S. Lewis made this comment about Satan and his fallen angels: "There are two equal and opposite errors into which our race can fall about the devils. One is to disbelieve in their existence. The other is to believe, and to feel an excessive and unhealthy interest in them. They themselves are equally pleased by both errors and hail a materialist or a magician with the same delight."[7]

Our Armor

4. Being told to put on God's armor can be somewhat daunting when we're not sure what it is and how to put it on. But we are urged to "put on every piece of God's armor so you will be able to resist the enemy in the time of evil" (Ephesians 6:13). To get a better grasp of God's protection, study these verses that relate to the individual pieces of armor and write down how they help your understanding of being armored against the devices of evil.

The belt of truth (Ephesians 6:14)

John 14:6

John 17:17

Santifucation

The breastplate of righteousness (Ephesians 6:14)

Jeremiah 23:5-6

God put everything right

2 Timothy 3:16

1548.49

Feet covered with the gospel of peace (Ephesians 6:15)

John 14:27

876 Psalm 119:165

The shield of faith (Ephesians 6:16)

1738 Hebrews 12:2

1623 Romans 10:17

faith comes from hearing the message

The helmet of salvation (Ephesians 6:17)

1566 Acts 4:10-12

cornerstone
Salvation is found in
no one else

1699 1 Thessalonians 5:8

foot note
We must have Spiritual awareness

The sword of the Spirit (Ephesians 6:17)

1388 Matthew 4:4

1724 Hebrews 4:12

It is God's Word which teaches us how to put on Christ and His graces so that we are fitly armed. Never flatter yourself into thinking you can do without this priceless book. We have all known those who content themselves with a profession of Christ and a smattering of gifts and works, and do not wish to know if there is more to the Christian life. They are the ones whose graces freeze when winter winds buffet their souls. But the saint whose faith has been insulated from error by the truth of the gospel will be able to withstand all Satan's icy blasts.[8]

William Gurnall

5. The Word is the only offensive weapon of our armor. Read Matthew 4:1-11 and record how Jesus countered Satan when He was tempted in the wilderness. How does the Lord's use of the Word encourage you to resist Satan?

Our Prayers

6. After Paul specifically lists the pieces of armor, he entreats us to pray. E. M. Bounds reminded us, "Note carefully that the Christian's armour will avail him nothing, unless prayer be added. This is the pivot, the connecting link of the armour of God. This holds it together, and renders it effective."[9] Carefully read Ephesians 6:18 and write down how, when, and for whom we are to pray.

1681-82

Pray in the Spirit

Jude 20 - 1772 foot note

Just as we need to be strong in the Lord and wear God's protective armor all day, so we need to live always praying in the Spirit. The Holy Spirit will not come to us nor work within us just at certain times when we think we need His help. The Spirit comes to be our life-companion. He wants us totally in His possession at all times; otherwise He cannot do His work in us. When this truth is grasped, we will realize that it is possible to live always praying in the power of the Spirit. The Spirit will keep us in a prayerful attitude and make us realize God's presence. Our prayer will be the continual exercise of fellowship with God and His great love.[10]

Andrew Murray

---

7. a. "Praying for all the saints [believers]" (Ephesians 6:18, NIV) is a key to spiritual warfare. Read the wonderful story of intercession found in Acts 12:1-19 and record your thoughts about the necessity, the power, and the blessing of praying for one another.

1580

1552

b. Jesus' own high priestly prayer is found in John 17. As you read verses 20-21, record for whom He prayed and His requests.

Believers

Today there still is a great need for Christians to be drawn close together in the awareness of their being chosen by God. We need to understand our role as a holy priesthood ministering continually the sacrifice of praise and prayer. What can be done to foster the unity of the Spirit?

Nothing will help so much as the separation to a life of more prayer, praying specifically that God's people will demonstrate the unity in a life of holiness and love. That will be a living testimony to the world of what it means to live for God. . . .

Earnestly desire to bear this mark of the children of God. Resolve to carry this great distinction of the Christian — a life of intercession. Join with others who are committed to praying down a blessing upon His Church. Don't hesitate to give a quarter of an hour every day for meditation on some promise of God to His Church — and then plead with Him for its fulfillment. Unobservedly, slowly, but surely, you will become one with God's people, and receive the power to pray the prayer that accomplishes much.[11]

Andrew Murray

8. Oswald Chambers noted, "The saint who satisfies the heart of Jesus will make other saints strong and mature for God."[12] One way to strengthen others is to intercede for them. How have you been encouraged or challenged to change your view of prayer in regard to spiritual warfare?

Thoughts from an Older Woman

Years ago I was meditating on Ephesians 6:10-19. I knew the importance of the armor, but I was never really certain about whether I was always fully armored. As I prayed, I came to realize that putting on the armor was putting on Christ (staying connected to Him on a daily basis) and being in His Word. These disciplines are essential components that define abiding in Christ. I believe that abiding is the key to being fully armored. As William Gurnall wrote, "To be without Christ and His graces is to be without armour."[13]

As I became confident of what the armor was and the necessity to stand firm against the strategies of the devil, I was fully prepared to pray *against* Satan. I was taken by surprise, though, when I carefully read in verse 18 to "be persistent in my prayers for all believers everywhere." That was a great moment for me. For the first time I understood that one of the best ways to wage spiritual warfare is by praying *for* the saints. It changed my prayer life.

When I pray for my church and the body of Christ worldwide, I pray for what Jesus prayed for: unity in the Lord so that the world will believe in Christ. I pray the prayers that Paul prayed for the church, found in his epistles. When I pray for countries and places around the world, I pray first for the strength and boldness of the missionaries and the Christians who live there.

Our prayers for the saints always strengthen and encourage the body, but it must be noted that our prayers are not always answered the way we would like. The church prayed for Peter to be delivered and he was, but I am sure the church also prayed for the apostle James, who was imprisoned and killed before Peter was arrested (see Acts 12:2). A significant thought for me was that the prayers of the church helped to produce the great peaceful sleep Peter experienced while in prison.

There is an interesting conversation that Jesus had with Peter in Luke 22:31-32. The Lord told Peter that Satan had asked to sift him like wheat, yet He assured Peter of His prayer "that your faith should not fail." We indeed have an enemy who wants to sift us like wheat, so it is imperative that we remain strong in the Lord, putting on all of God's armor and praying at all times, in the Spirit, for one another's faith. We need to pray as Paul prayed for the church: "I pray that from his glorious, unlimited resources he will empower you with inner strength through his Spirit. Then Christ will make his home in your hearts as you trust in him. Your roots will grow down into God's love and keep you strong" (Ephesians 3:16-17).

I will never forget one day when I was feeling rather discouraged. I asked the Lord what I needed to do — confess, pray, be still? I didn't hear anything immediately, but after a little while, the "cloud" lifted. I asked God, "What happened? Why am I better?" His answer in my heart was, "Cynthia, someone prayed for you."

> The Christian's armour is made to be worn — no taking it off until you have finished your course. Your armour and your garment of flesh come off together.[14]
>
> *William Gurnall*

REFLECTION
Strengthened Through His Spirit to Stand Firm

I never tire of reading Moody's story of how God answered the prayers of one woman committed to pray. Truly "the earnest prayer of a righteous person has great power and produces wonderful results" (James 5:16). As Russell Kelfer observed, "Prayer is not a casual experience; it is spiritual warfare."

The apostle John's teaching found in 1 John 4:4 — "You, dear children, are from God and have overcome them, because the one who is in you is greater than the one who is in the world" (NIV) — gives us courage and needed assistance that we can engage in spiritual warfare by interceding for the body of Christ. In your journal you might find it helpful to pray for believers by recording some of the key prayers in the New Testament: Ephesians 1:16-17; 3:14-21; Philippians 1:9-11; Colossians 1:9-12; and 2 Thessalonians 1:11-12. Andrew Murray's suggestion to take a quarter hour to pray for the church is a good beginning in joining with others who are committed to praying down a blessing upon His church.

Are you convinced that you cannot do without the Word of God, His sword of the Spirit? To be strong in the Lord and to withstand Satan's icy blasts, you need to be a student of the Word — to read it, study it, memorize it, and pray it. Use your journal to record your insights from the Scriptures.

To become a woman of strength, it is essential that you stay fully armored in order to stand firm against all strategies of the devil not only for yourself but also for the body of Christ. The Lord has provided armor and He empowers you with inner strength so that you can stay alert, resist the enemy, and be persistent in prayer.

Charles Spurgeon reminds us: "Let us fight as if all depends on us, but let us look up and know that all depends on Him."[15]

PRAYER THOUGHT

Okay, Lord, I can do this: Empowered by Your Spirit, I will stay fully armored so that I can stand firm and pray at all times, for I can do everything through Christ, who gives me strength.

In the same way, prayer is essential in this ongoing warfare. Pray hard and long. Pray for your brothers and sisters. Keep your eyes open. Keep each other's spirits up so that no one falls behind or drops out.

Ephesians 6:18, MSG

SUGGESTED SCRIPTURE MEMORY: Ephesians 6:18

CHAPTER EIGHT

Strong Enough to Be Bold

For God has not given us a spirit of fear and timidity, but of power, love, and self-discipline. So never be ashamed to tell others about our Lord. And don't be ashamed of me, either, even though I'm in prison for him. With the strength God gives you, be ready to suffer with me for the sake of the Good News.

2 TIMOTHY 1:7-8

Since you are forgiven freely (Romans 8:32), for Christ's sake go and tell others the joyful news of pardoning mercy. Do not be content to keep this unspeakable blessing for yourself alone. Preach the story of the cross. Holy gladness and holy boldness will make you a good preacher, and all the world will be your pulpit.[1]

CHARLES SPURGEON

Parable of the Fishless Fishermen

"Jesus called out to them, 'Come, follow me, and I will show you how to fish for people!' And they left their nets at once and followed him" (Matthew 4:19-20).

There was a group called Fisherman's Fellowship. They were surrounded by streams and lakes full of hungry fish. They met regularly to discuss the call to fish, the abundance of fish, and the thrill of catching fish. One of them suggested they needed a philosophy of fishing. So the group carefully defined and redefined fishing and the purpose of fishing. They developed strategies and tactics.

Then they realized they had been going at it the wrong way. They had approached fishing from the point of view of the fisherman and not from the point of view of the fish. How do fish view the world? How does the fisherman appear to the fish? What do fish eat and when? These are good things to know.

So some of them began research studies and attended conferences on fishing. Some traveled to faraway places to study various kinds of fish with different habits. Some got PhDs in Fishology.

But no one had yet gone fishing.

So a committee was formed to send out fishermen. As prospective fishing places outnumbered the fishermen, the committee needed to determine priorities. A priority list of fishing places was posted on bulletin boards in all the fellowship halls.

Still no one was fishing.

A survey was launched to find out why. Most did not answer the questionnaire, but from those who did respond, it was discovered that some felt called to study fish, a few to furnish fishing equipment, and several to go around encouraging fishermen. What with all the meetings, conferences, and seminars, others simply didn't have time to fish.

Jake was a newcomer to the Fisherman's Fellowship. After one stirring meeting of the fellowship, Jake went fishing. He tried a few things, got the hang of it, and caught a choice fish. At the next meeting, he told his story and was honored for his catch; then they scheduled him to speak at all the fellowship chapters to tell how he did it.

Now because of all the speaking and his appointment to the board of directors of the Fisherman's Fellowship, Jake no longer had time to go fishing.

Soon he began to feel restless and empty. He longed to feel the tug on the line once again. He cut the speaking, resigned from the board, and said to a friend, "Let's go fishing." They did, just the two of them, and they caught fish.

The members of the Fisherman's Fellowship were many, the fish were plentiful, but the fishers were few.[2]

Faithful Witnesses

1. Jake was not one to keep the joyful news of pardoning mercy to himself. What exactly is this joyful news? Record what the following verses tell you.

Romans 3:21-26

2 Corinthians 5:16-21

Colossians 1:19-20

A human being is like a lock, a lock made with such wondrous precision that only one key will fit it, only one key can open it wide, and that key turns out to be the simplest, the most basic skeleton key of all: the cross. When the cross touches a human heart, that heart glides open like a great steel door swinging freely on oiled bearings. Nothing else can do this.[3]

Mike Mason

2. We are not to keep the good news to ourselves. What do these Scriptures teach you about your call as a witness for Christ?

Acts 1:8

Romans 10:14-15

> Jesus died for sinners; cannot we live for sinners? Where is our tenderness? Where is our love for Christ if we do not seek His honor in the salvation of sinners? Oh that the Lord would saturate us through and through with an undying zeal for souls.[4]
>
> *Charles Spurgeon*

3. The psalmists gladly proclaimed the Lord's salvation. How do these passages encourage you to be a zealous witness?

Psalm 40:9-10

Psalm 71:15-16

Psalm 96:2-3

---

4. Having a tender heart for those who do not know Christ personally is key to being a faithful witness. How do these verses express tenderness for the lost?

Psalm 119:136

Romans 9:1-5

1 Corinthians 9:19-23

> The gospel is fearless. It boldly proclaims the truth whether it is accepted or not. We must be equally faithful and unflinching. But the gospel is also gentle. . . . Some believers are sharper than a thorn on a hedge. This is not like Jesus. Let us win others by the gentleness of our words and acts.[5]
>
> *Charles Spurgeon*

5. Paul wrote about how he related to the lost in this way: "I didn't take on their way of life. I kept my bearings in Christ—but I entered their world and tried to experience things from their point of view. I've become just about every sort of servant there is in my attempts to lead those I meet into a God-saved life. I did all this because of the Message. I didn't just want to talk about it; I wanted to be *in* on it!" (1 Corinthians 9:20-23, MSG). In today's world, what are some ways you can keep your bearings in Christ, yet enter the world of the lost in order to share the good news?

Bold Witnesses

6. We have not been given a spirit of timidity, but of power. To be bold is to be fearless, courageous, and unafraid. After reading these verses, record your thoughts about why each of us should not be ashamed of the gospel.

Mark 8:38

Romans 1:16

2 Timothy 1:7-8

7. Paul wrote in 2 Corinthians 3:12, "Since this new way gives us such confidence, we can be very bold." Along with tenderness and boldness, what principles of sharing the gospel do these verses present?

Colossians 4:5-6

1 Thessalonians 2:4-8

1 Peter 3:13-17

> You can never give another person that which you have found, but you can make him homesick for what you have.[6]
>
> *Oswald Chambers*

8. Charles Spurgeon referred to a holy boldness. How do you see holy boldness portrayed in these passages?

Ephesians 6:19-20

Philippians 1:12-14

9. Peter and John were jailed and taken before the Sanhedrin for proclaiming the gospel. They were commanded not to teach or speak in the name of Jesus. They responded by saying, "We cannot stop telling about everything we have seen and heard." After being released, they prayed with the church, "And now, O Lord, hear their threats, and give us, your servants, great boldness in preaching your word" (Acts 4:20,29). Take time to meditate on these verses and ask the Lord to speak to you about how you can become a bold witness for Him. Write down what you sense He is telling you.

Thoughts from an Older Woman

Witnessing encompasses not only words but also our responses and reactions. In reality we are witnessing 24/7. Christian writer Philip Yancey conducted an interesting survey. Afterward he wrote,

> Recently I have been asking a question of strangers — for example, seatmates on an airplane — when I strike up a conversation. "When I say the words, 'evangelical Christian' what comes to mind?" In reply, mostly I hear political descriptions: of strident pro-life activists, or gay-rights opponents, or propos-

als for censoring the Internet. . . . Not once — *not once* — have I heard a description redolent of grace. Apparently that is not the aroma Christians give off in the world.[7]

Yancey has a good point. Our goal in witnessing is to at least give a good name to "evangelical Christian" and to be ready to share the gospel or give an answer for the hope that is within us (see 1 Peter 3:15).

Once I was at the post office during the Christmas rush hour. Knowing that I would have to wait in line, I brought something to read along with my packages. The young man next to me made the comment that I was wise in bringing a book. This prompted a good ten-minute conversation that included the fact that I write Bible studies for Christian women. He asked a couple of questions about the studies, and I talked briefly about the importance of faith and inquired about his faith. He was very engaging; we laughed and shared freely. I have never seen him again, but my prayer is that someday if he is ever seated next to Philip Yancey and is asked what his thoughts are about evangelical Christians, he will respond, "You know, one time I met an old lady in the post office who was a Christian and she wasn't half bad."

I think it is important to fly my Christian flag early. By that I mean the sooner I let people know that I am a Christian, the easier it becomes for me to witness about the Lord or answer questions. Because I write Bible studies, I have a natural way of letting others know that I am a believer. One conversation with a seatmate on a plane showed a unique way of introducing the Lord into a discussion. He had yet to know of my faith, but when I asked him what he did, he replied, "The Lord has me flying airplanes." So anyone could say, "The Lord has me raising children" or "The Lord has me teaching school." This way, if we don't have an opportunity to share the gospel clearly, we can leave some aroma of grace.

I have had some unique experiences of witnessing on airplanes. Because most of my flights are early in the morning, I usually have my

Bible out to read. At times I've been asked questions such as "Do you think Jonah was really swallowed by a whale?" and "Do you believe everything in the Bible?" We've had some interesting discussions, and whenever I've been able to share the gospel clearly, I send books and other materials to encourage their continued seeking.

It is helpful to have some leading questions to ask in order to guide the conversation toward the things of the Lord and the sharing of the good news. My husband, Jack, after he has had an opportunity to visit with individuals for a period of time, asks, "What do you do for yourself spiritually?" This has opened the door for interesting and meaningful conversations and often a sharing of the gospel. Another good question is "What has been a memorable spiritual experience for you?"

Communicating the gospel does not come easily for me. My courage and encouragement to do so are found in Matthew 4:19 where the Lord takes responsibility for showing me how to fish. My part is to follow Him, to always be ready to share, and to live in such a way that I make others homesick for what I have. As I spend time with Him, I am given the strength, the sensitivity, and the appropriate way to share His good news with holy gladness and holy boldness.

> Through thick and thin, keep your hearts at attention,
> in adoration before Christ, your Master. Be ready to
> speak up and tell anyone who asks why you're living
> the way you are, and always with the utmost courtesy.
>
> *1 Peter 3:15-16*, MSG

REFLECTION
Strengthened Through His Spirit to Be Bold

The fisherman parable continually challenges me. It is an honor to share the gospel, and it is a thrill to feel the "tug on the line." As Paul wrote to the Corinthian church, "I do everything to spread the Good News and share in its blessings" (1 Corinthians 9:23).

Take your journal and prayerfully answer the following questions: Am I humbled by the gospel in my own life? Am I ashamed to share the gospel? Does my heart break for those who don't know the Lord? Am I willing to let my life be an example of the living gospel? Am I always ready to acknowledge the joyful news of God's pardoning mercy in my life? Do I pray for opportunities to be used by God as His ambassador?

In the previous chapter we studied the importance of praying for one another. Jesus taught that we are to pray for laborers to go out into the field of the world and minister (see Matthew 9:38). I have discovered that one of the best ways to pray for our loved ones who do *not* know the Lord is to pray for the believers who interact with them to be gracious, bold ambassadors of the gospel.

As you pray for yourself and for others, pray for us all to have an undying zeal for souls. May you be a faithful fisherman who is counted among the "few" fishermen who catch fish because of the Spirit's strengthening power equipping you to do all things.

May your heart be as Paul's: "What matters most to me is to finish what God started: the job the Master Jesus gave me of letting everyone I meet know all about this incredibly extravagant generosity of God" (Acts 20:24, MSG).

 PRAYER THOUGHT

Okay, Lord, I can do this: Empowered by Your Spirit, I can share the good news with a holy boldness, for I can do everything through Christ, who gives me strength.

But the Lord stood with me and gave me strength so that I might preach the Good News in its entirety for all the Gentiles to hear.

2 Timothy 4:17

SUGGESTED SCRIPTURE MEMORY: 2 Timothy 1:7-8

CHAPTER NINE

Strong Enough to Be Christ's Bondslave

As slaves of Christ, do the will of God with all your heart.

Ephesians 6:6

True Christianity is not about adding Jesus to my life. Instead, it is about devoting myself completely to Him — submitting wholly to His will and seeking to please Him above all else. It demands dying to self and following the Master, no matter the cost. In other words, to be a Christian is to be Christ's slave.[1]

John MacArthur

John Newton — Slave, Slave-Trader, and Slave of Christ

John Newton, author of the beloved hymn "Amazing Grace," wrote the following inscription for his own tombstone:

> JOHN NEWTON, Clerk,
> once an Infidel and Libertine,
> a Servant of Slaves in Africa,
> was, by the Rich Mercy of

> our Lord and Savior Jesus Christ,
> preserved, pardoned, and appointed to preach
> the Faith he had long labored to destroy.[2]

John Newton was born in London in 1725. John went to sea with his father when he was eleven years old. As a very young man he tried to live a good life, even vowed to lead the Christian life as he endured life-threatening storms at sea, but ultimately failed in all his efforts to be godly. After leaving a bar one night, he was hit over the head, carried on board a man-of-war ship, and thrown into the hold. Realizing the ship was to be gone for five years, he deserted, was recaptured, and publicly flogged. John eventually was traded for a sailor on another ship, a slave ship. He worked for different slave traders but at one point was employed in Africa by a slave trader who handed him over to his African mistress and head slave, who treated him cruelly. Another slave trader was able to secure John's release, treated him well, and helped him to become rather wealthy. At this time, though, he lived in open sin and wickedness.

It was a storm at sea that God used to bring John to saving faith. Fearing for his life, John cried out for God's mercy. Upon reflection in his cabin he discerned that the Lord had spoken to him and he sensed God's grace. He later wrote these words:

> I saw One hanging on a tree,
> In agonies and blood,
> Who fixed His eyes of love on me,
> As near the cross I stood.[3]

Although John continued on the slave ships for a period of time, he began to teach himself Latin, Greek, and Hebrew. When he returned home, his life changed completely. He married and found a job inspecting and taxing ships. He read the best Christian books available and was acquainted with known Christian leaders: George

Whitfield, John Wesley, William Cowper, and William Wilberforce.[4] When friends suggested that he become a pastor, he agreed and served in the pastorate for forty-three years.

John Newton knew the harsh realities of earthly slavery, but after experiencing the amazing grace of God who "saved a wretch like me," he gladly became a slave of Christ.

Bought with a Price

1. The word *servant* tends to have more stature or prestige than the word *slave*. Inherent in the word *slave* is the idea of subjection; a slave has no rights. John MacArthur makes this clarification: "While it is true that the duties of *slave* and *servant* may overlap to some degree, there is a key distinction between the two: servants are *hired*; slaves are *owned*. Servants have an element of freedom in choosing whom they work for and what they do. The idea of servanthood maintains some level of self-autonomy and personal rights. Slaves, on the other hand, have no freedom, autonomy, or rights."[5] How do these verses express the "slave" aspect of your life in Christ?

   Romans 6:19-22

   1 Corinthians 7:22-23

   1 Peter 1:18-19

   Only Jesus

Jesus has paid the purchase price and freed us from the deadly power of sin. He has taken us into his household, and now we find our destiny by accepting his lordship. In becoming slaves, subject to the will of God, we become what God intended us to be.[6]

Lawrence O. Richards

---

2. After James and John asked Jesus if they could sit in the places of honor next to Him, Jesus made a distinction between a servant and a slave. Read Mark 10:41-44 and write down your understanding of the differences. (You might find it helpful to consult a dictionary.)

Becoming **great** in Christian leadership means becoming a **servant**. The Greek work *diakonos* refers to a person who waits on tables. But even more is required of a disciple. **Whoever wants to be first among you must be a slave to all.** A "slave" [Greek, *doulos*] is lower than a servant, has no rights, and does only his master's bidding.[7]

Voluntary Submission

3. The key to being a slave for Christ is understanding that our Master redeemed us from an oppressive slavery to sin and the law in order to free us to be wholly His. It is His love that draws us to yoke ourselves *voluntarily* to the One who is humble and gentle in heart. As Murray J. Harris observed, "The nature of any slavery is determined by the nature of the master. Who and what the master is determines the status of the slave, the attitude of the slave, and the significance of the slave's work."[8] Read Exodus 21:1-6 and write down what you discover about becoming a slave to a loving master.

Salvation is not merely deliverance from sin, nor the experience of personal holiness; the salvation of God is deliverance out of self entirely into union with Himself. . . . In our abandonment we give ourselves over to God just as God gave Himself for us, without any calculation.[9]

Oswald Chambers

4. "The Greek word *dou'los* ('bond-slave') is used with the *highest dignity* in the [New Testament] — namely, of believers who *willingly* live under Christ's authority as His devoted followers."[10] Each of the Scriptures that follow uses *doulos* to mean "a slave." What do

you learn about the heart-attitude or purpose of a *doulos* from the following Scriptures?

Luke 17:7-10

John 13:12-17

Romans 6:15-18

Galatians 1:10

> His bondage is true freedom. His yoke is easy and His burden is light. What He has required, He has also enabled by His grace. And He calls us to obey, not because He needs us but because He knows that we need Him. After all, it is only in relationship with Him that our souls can be satisfied. Only by delighting in Him can we experience true joy and eternal life.[11]
>
> *John MacArthur*

---

5. In his letter to the Philippian church, Paul began by saying, "This letter is from Paul and Timothy, slaves of Christ Jesus" (Philippians 1:1).

Throughout the New Testament, service to the Lord is emphasized. What "job description" is given for a bondslave in these passages?

Galatians 5:13-14

Galatians 6:9-10

Do good to all people

1 Peter 4:10-11

> The passion of Christianity is that I deliberately sign away my own rights and become a bond-slave of Jesus Christ.[12]
>
> *Oswald Chambers*

Fixing Our Eyes on Jesus

6. a. Murray J. Harris commented, "It is Christ's voluntary role as God's *doulos* that prevents the Christian's slavery from being a distasteful experience and makes it a privilege and honour."[13] What can you learn about serving from Jesus' example?

   Mark 10:45

John 8:28-29

Philippians 2:5-11

b. In Galatians, Paul wrote of our relationship to God as His children and heirs — no longer slaves to the law (see 4:4-7). Before going to the cross, Jesus spoke about our special relationship to Him (see John 15:14-17). Record your thoughts about how our friendship with Jesus and our desire to serve Him correlate to one another.

H. R. Reynolds explains Jesus' teaching in this way: "I have raised you by the intimacy of the relations into which I have drawn you from the position of slave to that of friend. You may be, you must be, my servants still: I am your Master and Lord; but you will be servants from a higher motive and a more enduring link and bond of union."[14]

7. After studying this chapter, record any Scriptures or thoughts that have spoken to your heart about being a bondslave for Christ. How can these insights begin to impact your perspective and responses in the way you are currently living and serving the Lord?

Thoughts from an Older Woman

The original title for this chapter was "Strong Enough to Be a Servant." As I began to read and research for this topic, I realized that the word *doulos* actually means "to serve as a slave." Although *doulos* occurs 124 times in the New Testament, most English Bibles prefer to use the word *servant*, instead of *slave*. Murray J. Harris suggests several reasons why translators tend to avoid using *slave*. This is his main thought: "Why perpetuate those disconcerting memories by enshrining in the holy Scriptures an institution that has always deserved to be abhorred? . . . If *doulos* is rendered 'slave,' there is the ever-present danger that readers will project their first-hand knowledge of modern slavery back into the first century when slavery had a considerably different complexion."[15]

Nonetheless, the 124 times *doulos* is used, the New Testament writers were using the word *slave*. In the first question of this chapter, John MacArthur noted the difference between a slave and a servant. Harris made this further observation: "Every slave is a servant in that he or she is obligated to do the bidding of a superior; but not every servant is a slave. . . . The slave, being another person's property, does not have the servant's right to discontinue service."[16]

Years ago I went to speak at a weekend retreat that was held at a fairly rustic camp. I was taken to my room, which had a wooden frame bed with a green plastic mattress, a small desk, and a chair. Folded on top of the mattress I found a blanket, two flat sheets, a pillow, and one bath towel. I picked up my bedding, sat on the bed, looked at this stark room with no amenities, no bathroom, and only one towel and said to the Lord, "I am the speaker!" (I was ready to discontinue my service!) In the quietness, His voice reverberated in my heart in such a way that I can clearly hear His words today, "Oh, Cynthia, I thought you were My bondslave, who willingly does My bidding as My devoted follower."

I learned that day, in a singular way, that because I am truly God's *slave,* then I do His bidding when, where, and with what is available. I realized that God wants my heart before He wants my work. I understood that I do not determine the conditions under which I am to be used; I serve with the one towel given. Understanding that I am Christ's *doule* (female slave or bondmaid)[17] puts a whole different perspective on what service is. Because I have given my life to Him, I should respond to all that comes into my life (and particularly all "unwanted" assignments) as His bondslave, willing to do whatever He asks.

Oswald Chambers provides a good summary of this chapter:

To have a master and to be mastered is not the same thing. To have a master means that there is one who knows me better than I know myself, one who is closer than a friend, one who fathoms the remotest abyss of my heart and satisfies it, one who has brought me into the secure sense that he has met and solved every perplexity and problem of my mind. To have a master is this and nothing less — He wants us in the relationship in which He is easily Master without our conscious knowledge of it, all we know is that we are His to obey.[18]

In the summer of 1965, I surrendered my life to Christ. I placed my ear on the doorpost and asked the Lord to pierce it. I did it because I wanted to serve my Master for life. I did it because I love Him. I did it because I always want to be in the center of His will. I did it because of His amazing grace.

> Our Lord never insists on our obedience. He stresses very definitely what we *ought* to do, but He never *forces* us to do it. . . . If my relationship to Him is that of love, I will do what He says without hesitation. If I hesitate, it is because I love someone I have placed in competition with Him, namely, myself.[19]
>
> *Oswald Chambers*

REFLECTION
Strengthened Through His Spirit to Be a Slave for Christ

John Newton knew all about slavery, and once He met His true Master, he wholeheartedly and unreservedly was His slave. Mary, the mother of Jesus, was also wholeheartedly and unreservedly the Lord's. When Mary was told she would give birth to Jesus, she responded to the angel Gabriel by saying, "I am the Lord's slave . . . May it be done to me according to your word" (Luke 1:38, HCSB). Mary wholeheartedly trusted God with her life. She was His *doule,* available to do His will. She exemplified this thought from Oswald Chambers: "The passion of Christianity is that I deliberately sign away my own rights and become a bond-slave of Jesus Christ."[20]

Take some time and meditate on the Scriptures, quotations, and thoughts in this chapter. Go before the Lord and listen to what He has to say about whether you are a servant or a slave in His house. Ponder these questions: Are you willing to be Christ's *doule*? Can you trust God with your life? Can you embrace the concept of being Christ's slave and not just His servant? Are you willing to place your ear on the doorpost?

My prayer is that this chapter has challenged your view of what it is to be a bondslave to the Lord. It is not, "Okay, I'm going to do this project or I will serve for this length of time." It is devoting yourself completely to Him to be used as He pleases. When we are slaves of Christ, we serve 24/7, doing the will of God with all our hearts.

 PRAYER THOUGHT

Okay, Lord, I can do this: Empowered by Your Spirit and as a slave of Christ, I will do Your will with all my heart, for I can do everything through Christ, who gives me strength.

As soon as I pray, you answer me;
    you encourage me by giving me strength.

Psalm 138:3

SUGGESTED SCRIPTURE MEMORY: Ephesians 6:6

CHAPTER TEN

Strong Enough to Persevere

We also pray that you will be strengthened with all his glorious power so you will have all the endurance and patience you need.

COLOSSIANS 1:11

Do your afflictions seem as thick as the undergrowth confronting someone hiking through a jungle? Then take heart! Your time is not wasted, for God is simply putting you through His iron regimen. Your iron crown of suffering precedes your golden crown of glory, and iron is entering your soul to make it strong and brave.[1]

F. B. MEYER

Derek Redmond — One Who Persevered Through Hardships

Derek Redmond, a twenty-six-year-old Briton, was favored to win the 400-meter race in the 1992 Barcelona Olympics. During his career, he held the British record for the 400-meter sprint and won gold medals in the 4×400-meter relay at the World Championships, the European Championships, and the Commonwealth Games. Despite numerous operations on his Achilles tendon over the years, he felt confident as he began to run in the semifinal race.

Halfway around the track, a fiery pain seared through his right leg. He crumpled to the track with a torn hamstring. As medical attendants were approaching, Redmond fought to his feet. He set out hopping, pushing away the coaches in a crazed attempt to finish the race. London's *The Guardian* newspaper quoted him: "Everything I had worked for was finished. I hated everybody. I hated the world; I hated hamstrings; I hated it all. I felt so bitter that I was injured again. I told myself I had to finish. I kept hopping round. Then, with 100 metres to go, I felt a hand on my shoulder. It was my old man."[2] Jim Redmond, Derek's father, had barged past security and onto the track to get to his son.

"You don't have to do this," he told his weeping son.

"Yes, I do," Derek declared.

"Well, then," said Jim, "we're going to finish this together."[3]

Jim wrapped Derek's arm around his shoulder and just before they reached the finish line, with 65,000 spectators screaming in support, Jim Redmond let his son go, so that he could cross the finish line on his own.

God's Strength

1. Redmond personified spiritual perseverance by not giving up, by determining to stay the course, and by showing his dependence upon his father. Just as Derek's father watched his son run his race and came to his aid when needed, so our Father watches over and cares for us. How do these Scriptures confirm God's faithfulness in helping us, His children, endure trials?

Psalm 34:17-20

Psalm 46:1-3

1 Peter 5:10-11

Finally we learn, as the apostle Paul did with his thorn in the flesh, that God's grace is sufficient for us (2 Corinthians 12:9), however difficult and frustrating our circumstances might be. That is, God's *enabling* grace will give us the inner spiritual strength we need to bear the pain and endure the hardship, until the time when we see the harvest of righteousness and peace produced by it.[4]

Jerry Bridges

---

2. Charles Spurgeon prayed, "Oh my soul, what can destroy you if Omnipotence is your helper? If the protection of the Almighty covers you, what weapon can harm you?"[5] How is God's strength, protection, or comfort expressed in the following verses?

Psalm 23

Psalm 27:1-3

Isaiah 43:1-3

> Commentator E. Hurndall observed, "Our perfect helplessness is demonstrated, and then faith lays hold of God's perfect helpfulness. . . . The soul cries out for God, and can rest upon nothing but omnipotence. This is Christian life — despairing of our own power, confident in God's."[6]

3. "The Greek word *hypomenō* means 'to patiently endure.' In the Bible it usually has an active sense. Perseverance is overcoming difficulties; it is facing pressure and trials that call for a steadfast commitment to doing right and maintaining a godly life."[7] Think back over your life and recount a time when you sensed God's strength, protection, or comfort in overcoming your difficulties.

Our Perseverance

4. Isaiah 50:10 tells us, "If you are walking in darkness, without a ray of light, trust in the LORD and rely on your God." What do you learn about dealing with distress from the following prayers of Hannah and David?

1 Samuel 1:9-18

Psalm 61:1-5

Psalm 143

---

5. There was a time when King David was in a very difficult place. While David and his men were away, the Amalekites raided the town of Ziklag and carried off all their women and children. First Samuel 30:6 tells us, "David was now in great danger because all his men were very bitter about losing their sons and daughters, and they began to talk of stoning him. But David found strength in the LORD his God." By what means do you think David found strength in the Lord and how could this way give him strength? (Rereading his psalms cited in the previous questions might be helpful.)

---

6. Paul exhorted Timothy to "pursue righteousness and a godly life, along with faith, love, perseverance, and gentleness" (1 Timothy 6:11). After studying the following passages, express your thoughts concerning the value and ultimate blessing of perseverance.

Romans 5:3-5

2 Corinthians 1:8-10

James 1:2-4

Our Creator is not yet finished with us; He is still creating us, still making us, just as He has been all along from the beginning of the universe. But for the short span of our life here on earth we have the strange privilege of actually being wide awake as He continues to fashion us, to watch wide-eyed as His very own fingers work within our hearts. Of course this can be a painful process, and there is no anesthetic for it. At least, the only anesthetic is trust — trust in the Surgeon. But trust is not a passive, soporific thing. When there is a stabbing pain, trust cries out. It is only mistrust, fear, and suspicion that keep silent.[8]

Mike Mason

7. Trials and difficulties are tools in the hand of God. Read the following verses and write down the ways God honors your suffering.

2 Corinthians 4:16-18

James 1:12

1 Peter 1:6-7

---

8. The author of Hebrews wrote these words: "We who have fled to him for refuge can have great confidence as we hold to the hope that lies before us. This hope is a strong and trustworthy anchor for our souls" (6:18-19). If we desire to endure with patience, then hope must be our anchor. How do these verses encourage you and give you hope?

Psalm 33:20-22

Habakkuk 3:17-19

Romans 15:13

The trials and sorrows of life serve but to break up the fallow ground (Jer. 4:3); and without them our hearts would remain hard as the roadway; and the good seed, which may spring up to eternal life, would lie unheeded upon the surface, and find no entrance into their depths.[9]

R. Payne Smith

---

9. Someone observed, "Who can estimate the great debt we owe to suffering and pain?"[10] As you review this chapter, write a paragraph expressing your thoughts about how the Lord uses trials to strengthen us.

Thoughts from an Older Woman

Perseverance is not a particularly happy word, but it is a strong word — full of iron. It implies making a conscious decision to face reality and to persist with hope. I think of the Lord's words found in Isaiah 50:7: "Because the Sovereign LORD helps me, I will not be disgraced. Therefore, I have set my face like a stone, determined to do his will. And I know that I will not be put to shame." These words illustrate the essence of persevering: God's help and strength, our hearts determined to do His will, and His assurance of victory.

I did not grow up in a Christian home. We went to church rather sporadically, but it was more social than biblical. My father was fun loving but also a borderline alcoholic. There were frequent hearty disagreements between my mom and dad, followed by days of silence, then somehow things went back to normal until the next episode. Many nights I cried myself to sleep.

When I was twelve years old, I was given an opportunity to ask Christ into my life and I responded without any reservation. Although I had very little spiritual teaching, I did have a heart for God. I think it was then that I began to learn to persevere. The Lord became my refuge, my safe place. When I was in pain, I cried out and He was there for me.

As I moved through the next thirty-seven years, it was the Lord who gave me the love and patience I needed to interact with my dad. Each time we were together, I sensed God encouraging me, "You can do this. My grace is all you need. I am the strength of your heart."

Hebrews 11 clearly details the lives of men and women who exercised great faith while facing compelling challenges. We read that some of them were tortured, some chained in prison, some escaped death by the edge of the sword. Yet verse 34 notes, "Their weakness was turned to strength." Their example of faith and endurance serves to encourage us to trust God to perfect His power in our weakness. Because we are surrounded by such a great cloud of witnesses, Hebrews 12:1-2 exhorts us, then, to run our race with the same endurance these faithful pioneers experienced.

My dad did come to know the Lord shortly before he died, but he was never spiritually sensitive enough to help or encourage me in my race. Yet for the many years I have had to confront heartache and hard times, my heavenly Father has wrapped His arms around me and said, "I am here; we'll get through this together, for My strength is made perfect in your weakness."

There is another kind of patience that I believe is harder to obtain — the patience that runs. Lying down during a time of grief, or being quiet after a financial setback, certainly implies great strength, but I know of something that suggests even greater strength — the power to continue working after a setback, the power to still run with a heavy heart, and the power to perform your daily tasks with deep sorrow in your spirit. This is a Christlike thing![11]

George Matheson

REFLECTION
Strengthened Through His Spirit to Persevere

Sometimes it seems that we go through one iron regimen after another. Running with a heavy heart can become a way of life. We do need the iron of the Lord entering our soul to see us through to the golden crown of glory. We have to keep going — to persevere, to work — but we are "seen through" our trials through the power of the Holy Spirit. I think that Derek Redmond's experience illustrates in a symbolic way this truth: "Our part is to work, but to do so in reliance upon God to enable us to work. God's work does not make our effort unnecessary, but rather makes it effective."[12]

As you run your race, you can experience many "torn hamstrings" and the reality of performing your daily tasks with deep sorrow in your spirit. Perhaps there are times when you feel, as the psalmist David felt, that people are ready to throw rocks at you. Perhaps you are facing disease, troubled children, unemployment, failed relationships, and you feel the searing pain of hopelessness and helplessness.

This, above all times, is when you lean upon the Lord as your strong Shepherd who protects and comforts you with His rod and staff.

Keeping a journal and expressing your feelings in heartfelt prayers as Hannah and David did can be invaluable. Recording God's faithfulness to strengthen you in the midst of your trials helps you to remember His unfailing love, enabling grace, and glorious power to give you all the endurance and patience you need.

Seek His strength by running to Him as your fortress, your refuge in times of distress. Admit your helplessness by crying out to God and resting upon nothing but His omnipotence. You trust, you pray, you hope, you abide in Him. He, and He alone, is the strength of your heart. You can persevere because you can do all things through Christ who strengthens you.

 PRAYER THOUGHT

Okay, Lord, I can do this: Empowered by Your Spirit, I have all the endurance and patience I need, for I can do everything through Christ, who gives me strength.

 We are only promised strength according to our day, and not beyond the present day, in order that we may have a habit of reliance upon Christ for each day's strength.[13]

R. Finlayson

We pray that you'll have the strength to stick it out over the long haul — not the grim strength of gritting your teeth but the glory-strength God gives. It is strength that endures the unendurable and spills over into joy, thanking the Father who makes us strong enough to take part in everything bright and beautiful that he has for us.

Colossians 1:11-12, MSG

SUGGESTED SCRIPTURE MEMORY: Colossians 1:11

CHAPTER ELEVEN

Clothed With Strength

She is clothed with strength and dignity, and she laughs without fear of the future.

PROVERBS 31:25

When Jesus Christ enables me, I am omnipotently strong all the time.[1]

OSWALD CHAMBERS

Ruth Bell Graham — A Woman Who Clothed Herself with Strength

Ruth Bell was born in 1920 in China. Her parents were medical missionaries at a Presbyterian hospital three hundred miles north of the city of Shanghai. Even as a young girl her heart for the Lord was evident to those around her, and she sensed God calling her to abandon all for the sake of the gospel.

At age thirteen, she was sent to a boarding school in northern Korea where she was terribly homesick. "I spent most of my high school years in Korea. I didn't realize then that this initial separation from my parents would serve as my 'spiritual boot camp' for the years ahead."[2]

She wrote, "By 1937 I had my future securely planned. I would never marry. I would spend the rest of my life as a missionary in Tibet."[3]

Ruth attended Wheaton College in the United States, and it was there that she met "Preacher," the nickname the students had given to Billy Graham. They began dating and after agonizing in prayer over her call to be a missionary, she felt led to join Billy in his passion for evangelism. They were married in 1943. In her journal she made this prediction: "After the joy and satisfaction of knowing that I am his by rights — and his forever, I will slip into the background. . . . In short, be a lost life. Lost in Bill's."[4]

When Billy began traveling to conduct his evangelistic crusades, Ruth moved to Montreat, North Carolina, to be near her parents. There she established the family homestead and raised their five children.

As a wife, Ruth treasured her role as the strong woman behind America's pastor and was Billy's closest confidant, trusted adviser, and dearest friend. She was an avid reader, and many of the examples in Billy's sermons are from books she shared with him. He once commented, "She seems to know something about everything. Some of my best thoughts come from her."[5]

She looked for adventure. In her fifties, she took up hang gliding. After becoming a grandmother, she borrowed her son's leather jacket and took off on a Harley-Davidson motorcycle winding up in a ditch once and a lake another time.[6]

Ruth also had a wonderful sense of humor. There was a wooden sign above the door frame of her bedroom that said, "Nobody knows the trouble I've been."[7] And she proposed her own epitaph: "End of Construction: Thank you for your patience."[8] At age eighty-seven her "construction" came to an end and she went to be with her Lord.

During her lifetime, Ruth was an author and a poet. Here is a glimpse at one of her prayers: "Lord, the psalmist prayed, 'Give Your strength to Your servant' (Psalm 86:16), and my heart echoes his prayer. Not just spiritual strength, but plain old physical strength."[9]

Ned, Ruth's youngest son, made this observation about her: "With mother, I have seen true righteousness in a human being on a level that I've never seen before. There is absolutely no insecurity in the woman. There is total and absolute peace and confidence of who she is in God through Christ. There is a complete dependence and openness to the work of the Holy Spirit in her life. She hungers and thirsts after righteousness constantly. I've never seen anybody like it."[10]

Ruth Bell Graham exemplifies a woman of strength who was wholeheartedly committed to her Lord and who clothed herself with strength and dignity.

Clothing Our Spirit

1. Ruth Graham's life was a testimony to God's enabling strength. How do these verses confirm God's commitment to keep us strong?

Pg 828 Psalm 68:35   *gives strength & power*

1037 Isaiah 41:10   *give you strength & uphold*

1633 1 Corinthians 1:7-9

2. Although the Proverbs 31 woman wore fine linen and purple (verse 22), the emphasis is on her character. After studying the

following passages, write down the spiritual clothing that we are to put on.

*162*Romans 13:11-14

*169*Colossians 3:12-14

Put on love

1 Timothy 2:9-10

1 Peter 3:3-4

---

3. The Proverbs 31 woman clothed herself with strength *and* dignity (verse 25). Using the dictionary, define *dignity* and write a few sentences about why you think dignity is coupled with strength.

She may safely wear elegant garments, who in character and bearing is elegant without their aid. If honour be your clothing, the suit will last a life-time, but if clothing be your honour, it will soon be worn thread-bare.[11]

William Arnot

Smiling at the Future

4. Written in the margin of one of my Bibles beside Proverbs 31:25, I found this thought. I'm not sure of the origin, but I am sure of the truth these words convey: "You cannot assail my ability to smile at tomorrow because I know there is a God who is with me tomorrow." What guidance and encouragement to smile at the future can you find in the following verses?

Psalm 5:11-12

Psalm 18:1-3,32

Psalm 27:4-6

She is not disquieted by any fear of what may happen, knowing in whom she trusts, and having done her duty to the utmost of her ability.[12]

W. J. Deane and S. T. Taylor-Taswell

---

5. Smiling and laughing indicate a joyful spirit. What do these passages teach about the source of joy and blessing?

Psalm 16:11

Psalm 28:7

Psalm 84:4-5

---

6. "You have given me greater joy than those who have abundant harvests of grain and new wine" (Psalm 4:7). What can you learn from these verses about how to be filled with joy?

Psalm 97:11-12

Proverbs 8:32-34

John 15:9-11

---

7. After the wall was rebuilt in Jerusalem in 443 BC and the Israelites had settled in their towns, all the people assembled to hear Ezra read from the Book of the Law of Moses. The Levites also read and helped the people understand each passage. Read Nehemiah 8:9-12 (particularly note verse 10) and express your thoughts concerning how the joy of the Lord can be our strength.

"The joy of the Lord is *your* strength." Literally, your stronghold, fortress. For the Jews at this time, feeble as they were, the joy of the Lord would be safety against enemies. It would unite them, inspirit them, make them brave, stimulate them in God's service, which was their safety, as it would secure his protection and blessing. And in all times religious, holy joy is a defense against evil. . . . Against discouragement and despondency in trying times. Against sin. Making God's service a delight, it counterweighs the attractions of sinful pleasure.[13]

W. Clarkson

Thoughts from an Older Woman

An acrostic is usually a short poem in which the first letters of each sentence form a word. Proverbs 31:10-31 is an alphabetical acrostic where the initial letters of each verse are arranged in the order of the Hebrew alphabet. An acrostic is a common mnemonic learning device. I decided to take our eleven chapters, briefly summarize the content, and alphabetize the key thought of each chapter. Hopefully, this alphabetical arrangement will help you remember the topics that have been studied.

Chapter One: **A**bsolute Commitment — relying on God's strength alone
absolute: certain, whole, total

Chapter Two: **B**lessed Weakness — where His strength is most effective
blessed: fortunate, beneficial, exultant

Chapter Three: **C**ontinual Teachability — admitting my need for guidance and strength
continual: uninterrupted, ceaseless, constant

Chapter Four: **D**aily Waiting — gaining fresh strength
daily: everyday, habitual, customary

Chapter Five: **E**arnest Self-Control — strength to be Spirit-controlled
earnest: fervent, sincere, heart-felt

Chapter Six: **F**aithful Holiness — strength to be blameless
faithful: conscientious, virtuous, incorruptible

Chapter Seven: **G**allant Spiritual Warfare — strength to stand firm and to pray
gallant: brave, courageous, steadfast

Chapter Eight: **H**umble Boldness — strength in sharing the good news
humble: gracious, polite, respectful

Chapter Nine:	Intentional Slave of Christ — strength to serve unreservedly *intentional:* purposeful, voluntary, deliberate
Chapter Ten:	Jubilant Perseverance — relying on His glorious power to endure *jubilant:* triumphant, rejoicing, cheerful
Chapter Eleven:	Keen to Be Clothed with Strength — adorned with joyful strength *keen:* eager, intent, diligent

The Proverbs 31 woman's inner spirit was clothed with strength and dignity. I like the word *dignity* — noble bearing, worthiness, respectability. When I think of a woman who is dignified, I think of one who is gracious and has inherent nobility and worth. She is not full of herself; she understands that it is not "all about her." She is humble, teachable, patient, bold, and strong all at the same time. She is very aware that without the Lord she is helpless. It is this reliance on God's unlimited resources that enables her to clothe herself with strength and thereby conduct herself with dignity and honor.

I leave this study amazed that God's majestic, omnipotent power is mine. I leave blessed that God searches the earth to show Himself mighty on my behalf. I leave encouraged that my weakness is really God's realm of strength. I leave humbled by God's personal commitment to counsel me and give me strength to serve Him unconditionally and unreservedly through waiting, interceding, witnessing, holy living, and persevering. I leave secure that I can do all things through Christ, who strengthens me. I leave knowing that out of His glorious grace, He empowers me to be who He wants me to be: a woman of strength for His use and His glory.

Doubt your own strength,
but never Christ's.[14]

William Gurnall

REFLECTION
Strengthened Through His Spirit to Be Clothed with Strength

I want to close with two special quotations by Andrew Murray and Charles Spurgeon. I hope that they inspire your reflection and prayer.

God as the ever-living, ever-present, ever-acting One, who upholds all things by the word of His power, and in whom all things exist, meant that the relationship of His creatures to himself would be one of unceasing, absolute dependence. As truly as God by His power once created all things, so by that same power must God every moment maintain all things. We as His creatures have not only to look back to the origin and beginning of our existence and acknowledge that we owe everything to God—our chief care, highest virtue, and only happiness, now and throughout all eternity—but we must also present ourselves as empty vessels, in which God can dwell and manifest His power and goodness.[15]

Andrew Murray

Spend much time in prayer. Spend even a greater time in holy adoration. Read the Scriptures earnestly and consistently. Watch your life carefully. Live near God. Take the best examples for your models. Let your speech be the fragrance of heaven. Let your heart be perfumed with affection for lost souls. Live so that everyone will know that you have been with Jesus.[16]

Charles Spurgeon

My prayer for you is that as a result of this study, you are richly blessed to know how much God wants to strengthen you, so much so that He searches the whole earth in order to bestow His strength. I pray that you will experience the sufficiency of God's grace and the power of His strength working in your weaknesses. I pray that you will commit, wait, seek, pray, persevere, and serve empowered by the inner strength that can be given only by the Holy Spirit. I pray that whenever you are faced with a difficulty, a challenge, a trial of any kind, you will confidently say, "Okay, Lord, I can do this." I pray that as you rely on God's omnipotent strength, you will experience a life that is lived with joy, peace, self-control, and hope. I pray that as you dress each morning, you will always remember to clothe yourself with strength and dignity. I pray that daily you will present yourself as an empty vessel so that out of His glorious, inexhaustible riches, He may strengthen you to do all things through Christ.

As you review your thoughts and prayers in your journal, take time to write a closing prayer of commitment to the Lord expressing gratefulness for what you have learned and practical ways you want to continue to become a woman of strength as well as stating your desire that from this day forth you want the Lord to enable you with His endless energy and boundless strength to live a life pleasing to Him.

 PRAYER THOUGHT

Okay, Lord, I can do this: Empowered by Your Spirit, I can become a woman who is clothed in the strength of my Almighty God and can therefore do everything through Christ, who gives me strength.

God — He clothes me with strength
and makes my way perfect.

Psalm 18:32, HCSB

SUGGESTED SCRIPTURE MEMORY: Proverbs 31:25

A final word: Be strong in the Lord and in his mighty power.

Ephesians 6:10

Your strength, O Lord, not mine I seek.
For Your power works best when I am weak.

The Father and the Child

The Father spoke:
Are you well, My child?
Yes, Father, I am well in my spirit.
It is good to see that you are learning to understand that I am your source of strength.
I am finding out in a new way that relying on Your strength serves to accomplish Your purposes in a far higher and more profitable way than depending on my strength or focusing on my weaknesses. I also understand that being empowered by Your strength doesn't necessarily make my journey any easier, but it does give me the capacity and confidence to live as Your child for Your glory.
The secret is to trust in the sufficiency of My grace, the completeness of My love, and the greatness of My strength.
I am humbled by Your bountiful provision for my needs. How often I pray for my surrender and wholeheartedness as I turn from independence to dependence, from trust in myself to trust in my Almighty Lord, from the ways of the world to the ways of Your kingdom, from token service to total commitment as Your bondslave, from haste and impatience to peaceful waiting, from timidity to boldness, from feeling powerless to knowing I am empowered to do all things.
Always know that I am the strength of your heart and your portion forever.
Thank You, Father, gladly I place my hand in Yours. Thank You that from Your glorious, unlimited resources You empower me with inner strength through Your Spirit. May I continue to see and hear Your Word, look to You for my daily strength, and proclaim to all, "The LORD is my strength and my song; he has given me victory" (Exodus 15:2).

Notes

Introduction

1. T. Croskery, *The Pulpit Commentary, Galatians–Colossians,* ed. H. C. M. Spence and Joseph S. Excell (Peabody, MA: Hendrickson, n.d.), 20:118.
2. "New Testament Greek Lexicon," Heartlight's Search God's Word, http://www.searchgodsword.org/lex/grk/search.cgi?word=dunamoo&search.x=0&search.y=0&search=Lookup.
3. Matthew Henry, *Commentary on the Whole Bible* (Iowa Falls, IA: Riverside, n.d.), 6:747.
4. W. F. Adeney, in *The Pulpit Commentary, Galatians–Colossians,* 20:198.
5. Jerry Bridges, *The Discipline of Grace* (Colorado Springs, CO: NavPress, 1994), 132.
6. Croskery, 267.

Chapter One: God, the Great Giver of Strength

1. Oswald Chambers, *My Utmost for His Highest* (Westwood, NJ: Barbour, 1935), August 14.
2. Basil Miller, *Mary Slessor: Heroine of Calabar* (Minneapolis: Bethany House, 1946), 18.
3. Miller, 23.
4. Miller, 52–53.
5. Edith Deen, *Great Women of the Christian Faith* (Westwood, NJ: Barbour, 1959), 253.
6. Deen, 250.
7. W. P. Livingstone, *Mary Slessor of Calabar: Pioneer Missionary,* 8th ed. (New York: George H. Doran Co., 1917), in "Some Thoughts Written in Mary Slessor's Bible," Wholesome Words, http://www.wholesomewords.org/missions/bioslessor4.html.
8. Matthew Henry, *Commentary on the Whole Bible* (Iowa Falls, IA: Riverside, n.d.), 2:955.
9. Charles Spurgeon, *Morning and Evening: An Updated Edition of the Classic Devotional in Today's Language,* ed. Roy H. Clarke (Nashville: Thomas Nelson, 1994), November 21, morning.
10. E. M. Bounds, *The Complete Works of E. M. Bounds on Prayer* (Grand Rapids, MI: Baker, 1990), 118–119.
11. Spurgeon, November 4, morning.

Chapter Two: His Strength in Our Weakness

1. Charles Spurgeon, *Morning and Evening: An Updated Edition of the Classic Devotional in Today's Language*, ed. Roy H. Clarke (Nashville: Thomas Nelson, 1994), November 4, morning.
2. Doug Nichols, http://www.dougnichols.blogspot.com.
3. Phil Callaway, *Who Put My Life on Fast-Forward?* (Eugene, OR: Harvest House, 2002), 228–232.
4. Linda L. Belleville, *2 Corinthians*, IVP New Testament Commentary Series, ed. Grant R. Osbourne (Downers Grove: InterVarsity, 1996), http://www.biblegateway.com/resources/commentaries/IVP-NT/2Cor/Paul-Matches-Opponents.
5. Russell Kelfer, *God's Amazing Grace* (San Antonio, TX: Discipleship Tape Ministries, 2001), 90.
6. A. B. Simpson, in *Streams in the Desert*, comp. L. B. Cowman, ed. Jim Reimann (Grand Rapids, MI: Zondervan, 1997), April 8.
7. Belleville.
8. John Owen, in *The Westminster Collection of Christian Quotations*, comp. by Martin H. Manser (Louisville, KY: John Knox, 2001), 397.

Chapter Three: Strong Enough to Be Teachable

1. J. I. Packer, in *Never Scratch a Tiger with a Short Stick*, comp. Gordon Jackson (Colorado Springs, CO: NavPress, 2000), 79.
2. Kevin Belmonte, *Hero for Humanity* (Colorado Springs, CO: NavPress, 2002), 51.
3. Belmonte, 91.
4. Belmonte, 86.
5. Belmonte, 95.
6. Mike Mason, *The Gospel According to Job* (Wheaton, IL: Crossway, 1994), 229–230.
7. Oswald Chambers, *My Utmost for His Highest* (Westwood, NJ: Barbour, 1935), May 13.
8. Chambers, May 13.
9. Dawson Trotman, in *Never Scratch a Tiger with a Short Stick*, 53.
10. "Counselors," commentary in *New Living Translation Study Bible* (Carol Stream, IL: Tyndale, 2008), 869.
11. A. C. Hervey, *The Pulpit Commentary, Acts/Romans*, eds. H. C. M. Spence and Joseph S. Excell (Peabody, MA: Hendrickson, n.d.), 18:170.
12. Anonymous, in *Streams in the Desert*, comp. L. B. Cowman, ed. Jim Reimann (Grand Rapids, MI: Zondervan, 1997), December 4.

Chapter Four: Strong Enough to Wait

1. Samuel Dickey Gordon, in *Streams in the Desert,* comp. L. B. Cowman, ed. Jim Reimann (Grand Rapids, MI: Zondervan, 1997), August 16.
2. E-mail from Lorraine Scobel, January 5, 2011.
3. Martha Snell Nicholson, "The Thorn," Suffering Christians (blog), http://www.scripturezealot.com/sufferingchristians/2010/02/03/the-thorn/.
4. John Trapp, in Charles Spurgeon, *Treasury of David* (McLean, VA: MacDonald Publishing, n.d.), 2:54.
5. Hudson Taylor, in *Worth Repeating,* comp. Bob Kelly (Grand Rapids, MI: Kregel, 2003), 362.
6. Oswald Chambers, *My Utmost for His Highest* (Westwood, NJ: Barbour, 1935), January 4.
7. "The Still Small Voice," in *Streams in the Desert,* September 5.
8. Andrew Murray, *The Believer's Secret of Waiting on God* (Minneapolis: Bethany House, 1986), 40, 99.
9. Murray, 95.
10. Phillips Brooks, in *Quotes for the Journey, Wisdom for the Way,* comp. Gordon S. Jackson (Colorado Springs, CO: NavPress, 2000), 20.
11. Selected, *Streams in the Desert,* March 22.
12. Charles Spurgeon, *Morning and Evening: An Updated Edition of the Classic Devotional in Today's Language,* ed. Roy H. Clarke (Nashville: Thomas Nelson, 1994), February 14, morning.
13. Spurgeon, September 28, evening.
14. Gordon, October 14.
15. Peter Marshall, in *The Westminster Collection of Christian Quotations,* comp. by Martin H. Manser (Louisville, KY: John Knox Press, 2001), 270.
16. George Matheson, in *Streams in the Desert,* April 8.
17. From *Morning by Morning,* in *Streams in the Desert,* November 20.

Chapter Five: Strong Enough to Exercise Self-Control

1. E. Johnson, *The Pulpit Commentary, Proverbs/Ecclesiastes/Song of Solomon,* ed. H. C. M. Spence and Joseph S. Excell (Peabody, MA: Hendrickson, n.d.), 9:324.
2. Excerpted from "The Story of Carl," http://www.thelordsprayer.net/carl.html.
3. J. Willcock, in *The Pulpit Commentary, Proverbs/Ecclesiastes/Song of Solomon,* 9:193.
4. Reverend Kevin Rietveld, in *Solomon Star News,* http://www.solomonstarnews.com/features/religion/4517-thought-for-the-week-fruitful-lives--self-control.

5. Jack Wisdom, "Self-Mastery and the Imperishable Prize," *Christianity Today*, http://www.christianitytoday.com/workplace/articles/leadership/selfmastery.html.

6. "Way of Faith," in *Streams in the Desert*, comp. L. B. Cowman, ed. Jim Reimann (Grand Rapids, MI: Zondervan, 1997), October 3.

7. Jerry Bridges, "Self-Control Quotes," oChristian.com, http://christian-quotes.ochristian.com/Self-control-Quotes.

8. A. B. Simpson, in *Streams in the Desert*, March 18.

9. C. S. Lewis, *Prince Caspian* (New York: HarperCollins, 1951), 149.

10. A. B. Simpson, in *Streams in the Desert*, October 6.

11. Johann Friedrich Lobstein, in *The Westminster Collection of Christian Quotations*, comp. Martin H. Manser (Louisville, KY: John Knox Press, 2001), 334.

Chapter Six: Strong Enough to Be Holy

1. Jerry Bridges, *The Pursuit of Holiness* (Colorado Springs, CO: NavPress, 1978), 78.

2. Russell Kelfer, *God's Amazing Grace* (San Antonio, TX: Discipleship Tape Ministries, 2001), 96–97.

3. Oswald Chambers, *My Utmost for His Highest* (Westwood, NJ: Barbour, 1935), October 6.

4. Jerry Bridges, *The Discipline of Grace* (Colorado Springs, CO: NavPress, 1994), 134.

5. Bridges, *Discipline of Grace*, 61.

6. Chambers, March 21.

7. Chambers, April 11.

8. Chambers, April 15.

9. Charles Spurgeon, *Morning and Evening: An Updated Edition of the Classic Devotional in Today's Language*, ed. Roy H. Clarke (Nashville: Thomas Nelson, 1994), March 11, morning.

10. Mike Mason, *The Gospel According to Job* (Wheaton, IL: Crossway, 1994), 258.

11. John Murray, in *The Gospel According to Job*, 102.

12. J. C. Ryle, in *The Sufferings of Christ Jesus: Keep Me Near the Cross*, ed. Nancy Guthrie (Wheaton, IL: Crossway, 2009), 58.

Chapter Seven: Strong Enough for Spiritual Warfare

1. Russell Kelfer, *God's Amazing Grace* (San Antonio, TX: Discipleship Tape Ministries, 2001), 136.

2. R. A. Torrey, *The Power of Prayer and the Prayer of Power* (Grand Rapids, MI: Zondervan, 1971), 36.

3. Torrey, 37.

4. Torrey, 38.

5. Paul Thigpen, "Our Weaponry," *Discipleship Journal* (May/June 2006), http://www.navpress.com/magazines/archives/ search.aspx?theme=&type =simple&q=Spiritual+Warfare.

6. "The Old Life and the New Life," commentary in *New Living Study Bible* (Carol Stream, IL: Tyndale, 2008), 2005.

7. C. S. Lewis, *The Screwtape Letters* (New York: Macmillan, 1958), 9.

8. William Gurnall, *The Christian in Complete Armour*, vol. 1 (Carlisle, PA: The Banner of Truth Trust, 1986), 66.

9. E. M. Bounds, *The Necessity of Prayer* (Grand Rapids, MI: Baker, 1976), 115.

10. Andrew Murray, *The Best of Andrew Murray on Prayer: A Daily Devotional on the Deeper Christian Life* (Uhrichsville, OH: Barbour, 2000), May 5.

11. Murray, July 16.

12. Oswald Chambers, *My Utmost for His Highest* (Westwood, NJ: Barbour, 1935), August 10.

13. Gurnall, 60.

14. Gurnall, 76.

15. Charles Spurgeon, *Morning and Evening: An Updated Edition of the Classic Devotional in Today's Language*, ed. Roy H. Clarke (Nashville: Thomas Nelson, 1994), April 20, evening.

Chapter Eight: Strong Enough to Be Bold

1. Charles Spurgeon, *Morning and Evening: An Updated Edition of the Classic Devotional in Today's Language*, ed. Roy H. Clarke (Nashville: Thomas Nelson, 1994), August 14, morning.

2. Fish the Net (http://www.fishthe.net/fishless.htm) cites the parable as anonymous, but with further research, I found that other sources attribute the parable to Pastor John Drescher.

3. Mike Mason, *The Gospel According to Job* (Wheaton, IL: Crossway, 1994), 326.

4. Charles Spurgeon, Wholesome Words, http://wholesomewords.org.

5. Spurgeon, *Morning and Evening*, December 7, evening.

6. Oswald Chambers, *My Utmost for His Highest* (Westwood, NJ: Barbour, 1935), June 10.

7. Philip Yancey, *What's So Amazing About Grace?* (Grand Rapids, MI: Zondervan, 1997), 31.

Chapter Nine: Strong Enough to Be Christ's Bondslave

1. John MacArthur, *Slave: The Hidden Truth About Your Identity in Christ* (Nashville: Thomas Nelson, 2010), 22.
2. Christopher Knapp, "John Newton," Wholesome Words, http://www.wholesomewords.org/biography/bnewton9.html.
3. Knapp.
4. "Biography of John Newton," Christian Classics Ethereal Library, http://www.ccel.org/n/newton.
5. MacArthur, 16–17.
6. Lawrence O. Richards. *Expository Dictionary of Bible Words* (Grand Rapids, MI: Regency Reference Library, 1985), 554.
7. Russ H. McLaren, commentary note on Mark 10:43-44, *Holman Christian Study Bible* (Nashville: Holman Bible Publishers, 2010), 1704–1705.
8. Murray J. Harris, *Slave of Christ: A New Testament Metaphor for Total Devotion to Christ* (Downers Grove, IL: InterVarsity, 1999), 135.
9. Oswald Chambers, *My Utmost for His Highest* (Westwood, NJ: Barbour, 1935), March 13.
10. http://www.strongnumbers.com/greek/1401.
11. MacArthur, 208.
12. Chambers, November 3.
13. Harris, 137.
14. H. R. Reynolds, *The Pulpit Commentary, John* (Peabody, MA: Hendrickson, n.d.), 17 (vol. 2):272.
15. Harris, 184.
16. Harris, 187.
17. http://www.strongnumbers.com/greek/1399.
18. Chambers, September 22.
19. Chambers, November 2.
20. Chambers, November 3.

Chapter Ten: Strong Enough to Persevere

1. F. B. Meyer, in *Streams in the Desert*, comp. L. B. Cowman, ed. Jim Reimann (Grand Rapids, MI: Zondervan, 1997), December 27.
2. "Derek Redmond," Sports Feel Good Stories, http://www.sportsfeelgoodstories.com/index.php?s=derek+redmond.
3. Phil McCallum, "The Derek Redmond Story," Deeper Still, http://www.philmccallum.com/2007/12/14/the-derek-redmond-story.
4. Jerry Bridges, *The Discipline of Grace* (Colorado Springs, CO: NavPress, 1994), 231.

5. Charles Spurgeon, *Morning and Evening: An Updated Edition of the Classic Devotional in Today's Language*, ed. Roy H. Clarke (Nashville: Thomas Nelson, 1994), April 21, evening.

6. E. Hurndall, *The Pulpit Commentary, 1 & 2 Corinthians*, eds. H. C. M. Spence and Joseph S. Excell (Peabody, MA: Hendrickson, n.d.), 19:21.

7. Lawrence O. Richards, *Expository Dictionary of Bible Words* (Grand Rapids, MI: Regency Reference Library, 1985), 484.

8. Mike Mason, *The Gospel According to Job* (Wheaton, IL: Crossway, 1994), 58.

9. R. Payne Smith, *The Pulpit Commentary, Ruth/1 & 2 Samuel*, 4:595.

10. Selected, in *Streams in the Desert*, August 10.

11. George Matheson, in *Streams in the Desert*, October 30.

12. Bridges, 133.

13. R. Finlayson, *The Pulpit Commentary, Galatians–Colossians*, 20:182.

Chapter Eleven: Clothed with Strength

1. Oswald Chambers, in *The Quotable Oswald Chambers*, comp. and ed. David McCasland (Grand Rapids, MI: Discovery House, 2008), 273.

2. Ruth Bell Graham, *Footprints of a Pilgrim: The Life and Loves of Ruth Bell Graham* (Nashville: Word, 2001), 34.

3. Graham, 37.

4. Graham, 66.

5. Joyce Vollmer Brown, *Courageous Christians: Devotional Stories for Family Reading* (Chicago: Moody, 2000), 82.

6. Brown, 82.

7. Laura Sessions Stepp, "Ruth Bell Graham: The Soul Mate of the Preacher," *Washington Post*, June 16, 2007, http://www.washingtonpost.com/wp-dyn/content/article/2007/06/15/AR2007061502363.html.

8. Ted Olsen, "Ruth Graham's Epitaph," CT Liveblog, *Christianity Today*, June 15, 2007, http://blog.christianitytoday.com/ctliveblog/archives/2007/06/ruth_grahams_ep.html.

9. Ruth Bell Graham, comp., *Prayers from a Mother's Heart* (Nashville: Thomas Nelson, 1999), 45.

10. Billy Graham, "Ruth Bell Graham: Memories," Billy Graham Evangelistic Association, http://www.billygraham.org/specialsections/rbg/RBG_Memories.asp.

11. William Arnot, *Laws from Heaven for Living on Earth* (London: T. Nelson, 1864), http://www.archive.org/stream/lawsfromheavenf02arnogoog#page/n578/mode/1up.

12. W. J. Deane and S. T. Taylor-Taswell, *The Pulpit Commentary, Proverbs/Ecclesiastes/Song of Solomon*, eds. H. C. M. Spence and Joseph S. Excell (Peabody, MA: Hendrickson, n.d.), 9:601.

13. W. Clarkson, *The Pulpit Commentary, Ezra/Nehemiah/Esther/Job*, 7:84.

14. William Gurnall, *The Christian in Complete Armour*, vol. 1 (Carlisle, PA: The Banner of Truth Trust, 1986), 65.

15. Andrew Murray, *Humility* (Minneapolis: Bethany House, 2001), 15.

16. Charles Spurgeon, *Morning and Evening: An Updated Edition of the Classic Devotional in Today's Language*, ed. Roy H. Clarke (Nashville: Thomas Nelson, 1994), March 14, morning.

About the Author

*C*ynthia Heald was born in Houston, Texas, and received Christ as her personal Savior when she was twelve years old. In 1960, Cynthia married Jack, who by profession is a veterinarian but has been on staff with The Navigators since 1978. They have lived in Tucson, Arizona, since 1977 and are the parents of four (two daughters and two sons) and grandparents of nine.

Cynthia is the author of *Becoming a Woman of Excellence, Becoming a Woman of Faith, Becoming a Woman of Freedom, Becoming a Woman of Grace, Becoming a Woman of Prayer, Becoming a Woman of Purpose, Becoming a Woman of Simplicity, Becoming a Woman Who Loves, Becoming a Woman Who Walks with God, Drawing Near to the Heart of God, Dwelling in His Presence, Intimacy with God, Loving Your Husband, Maybe God Is Right After All, Uncommon Beauty,* and *When the Father Holds You Close.*

Cynthia speaks frequently for women's conferences and seminars nationally and internationally. She loves to share the Word of God, be with her husband and family, take bubble baths, have tea parties, and eat out.

Use the study with the accompanying DVD!

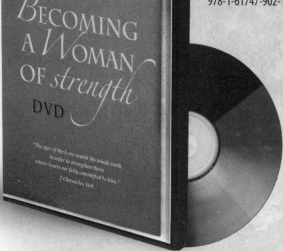

Becoming a Woman of Strength DVD
Cynthia Heald

In this eleven-session DVD, Cynthia Heald teaches you how to use the Holy Spirit for inner strength. Take your women's study through a powerful inner change of transformation.

978-1-61747-902-1

Sarah
Young
Jesus Calling